THOMAS WILLIAMS is the author of the bestselling and critically acclaimed *Viking Britain*. He was a curator of the major international exhibition Vikings: Life and Legend in 2014 and more recently a curator of early medieval coins at the British Museum. Educated at UCL, he is a fellow of the Society of Antiquaries of London and has taught at the University of Cambridge.

Also by Thomas Williams

Viking Britain

For children
The Tale of King Harald: The Last Viking Adventure

THOMAS WILLIAMS

VIKING LONDON

**WILLIAM
COLLINS**

William Collins
An imprint of HarperCollins*Publishers*
1 London Bridge Street
London SE1 9GF
WilliamCollinsBooks.com

First published in Great Britain in 2019 by William Collins
This William Collins paperback edition published in 2020

1

A catalogue record for this book is available from the British Library

ISBN 978-0-00-829989-7

Maps by Martin Brown

Typeset in Birka by
Palimpsest Book Production Ltd, Falkirk, Stirlingshire

Printed and bound in Great Britain by CPI Group (UK) Ltd, Croydon CR0 4YY

MIX
Paper from
responsible sources
FSC™ C007454

For Pru

Contents

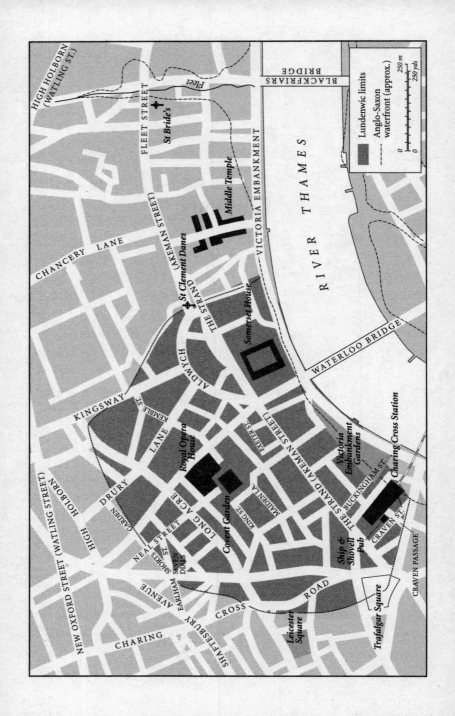

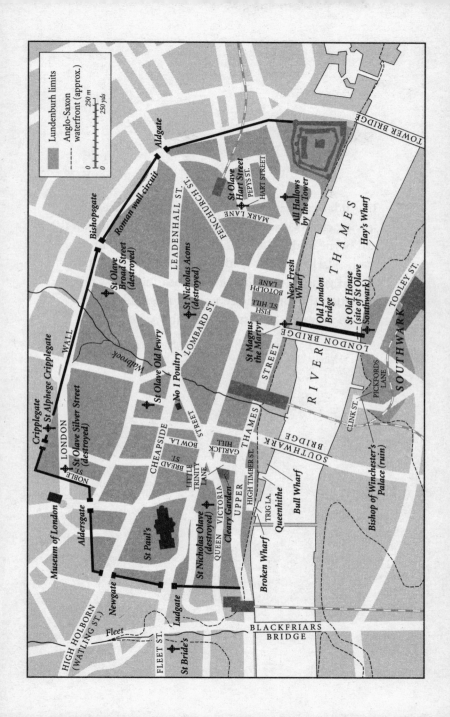

The tidal current runs to and fro in its unceasing service, crowded with memories of men and ships it had borne to the rest of home or to the battles of the sea [. . .] Hunters for gold or pursuers of fame, they all had gone out on that stream, bearing the sword, and often the torch, messengers of the might within the land, bearers of a spark from the sacred fire.

Joseph Conrad, *Heart of Darkness*

Introduction

Wherever their ships ploughed the water, the Vikings made needles of rivers: a hypodermic rush of systemic devastation and steroidal vigour, wracking the veins of nations with the germ of change. In Dublin, York and Kiev, Iceland, Normandy and Russia, the Vikings planted the seeds of new realms and great cities, stoking the furnaces of trade, technology and industry wherever their keels ground the shingle and markets echoed with the jangle of slave-chains. They remoulded the world for ever, violence and commerce riding the whale-road from the north: twin sea-stallions of the Viking Age. In Britain the impact was profound: the Vikings remade the geopolitical map, changed the language, up-ended the dynamics of power and trade. Monasteries and settlements burned, ancient dynasties were extinguished. And nowhere in these islands was subjected to more aggression than London.

Between 842 and 1016 London was assaulted by Vikings on at least a dozen separate occasions. Sometimes it burned and sometimes it surrendered, mostly it stood firm when all others had given up hope; and throughout it all the city endured, remaking and remodelling itself, growing strong in adversity, unique in economic power, a crucible of cultures, enterprise and political intrigue: a maker of kings, the heart of a North Sea empire. This book is a sketch of London in the Viking Age, how it remade itself, how it was transformed by immigrants and natives, kings and commoners into the fulcrum of national power and identity. London emerged as a hub of trade, production and international exchange, a financial centre, a political prize, a fiercely independent and often intractable cauldron of spirited and rowdy townsfolk: a place that, a thousand years ago, already embodied much of what London was to become and still remains.

This book is also, however, a confrontation with the city that still sprawls beside the Thames – a delving into its darkest age, an invasion of its privy parts.

Viking Age London is like an old wound, seemingly long healed and oft forgotten. But sometimes in the winter, when a cold wind blows from the north, it still nags – an ache that will never go away. Stumbling around corners, feet catch on stitches, pull back the skin of modernity – an ancient street name hidden beneath a concrete underpass, a paved void where a church no longer stands, a stretch of the old riverbank crawling out from beneath embankments. For nothing is lost in the city: things just sink further into the mire, deeper into time.

Occasionally, however, those memories break free,

bursting upward like the hands of hungry corpses, or shimmering wraith-like through the alluvium. They hover like a miasma in the crypts of old churches or the depths of museum collections, drifting amongst beer cans at the blood-coloured foot of London Wall or blowing across the mud and shingle on the Thames foreshore. In these places the ghosts of Viking London still assemble, the murmur of *liðsmen* mingling with the banter of Victorian antiquarians, the chatter of tourists, the profanities of drunks. London is a city of spectres, of ghosts walking in the footsteps of other ghosts, and the Viking Age is perhaps its most forgotten hinterland.

And through it all runs the river, that titanic, oily-backed serpent. It winds its monstrous coils through Viking London – through time and place, providing and devouring, poisoning and fattening – before unravelling, unbound, into a mess of estuarine chaos, its mighty body dissolving to the sea.

I

Lundenwic

The *Anglo-Saxon Chronicle* relates that in the year 842 'there was a great slaughter in London and in Quentovic and in Rochester'.[1] In an entry for the same year, the *Annals of St Bertin*, a chronicle compiled in what is now northern France, describes the raid on Quentovic, a trading centre just across the Channel, and names the antagonists as 'northmen'.[2] The Vikings had come to London.

By the 840s Viking raids had been a feature of British life for around half a century. The first raids occurred in Wessex and Northumbria at the end of the eighth century, but from the 830s onward Viking fleets had grown larger and the threat they posed more serious. West Saxon kings had faced Viking armies in pitched battle on a number of occasions; the king of Northumbria lost his life to a Viking raiding army in 844. The earliest raid on London that we know of is that of 842, but it was not necessarily the first.

Fifty years earlier, in 792, King Offa of Mercia – the Midland realm that at the time was the most powerful kingdom in southern Britain – had a charter drawn up confirming the exemption of Kentish churches from various obligations that landholders normally owed to their royal overlords. It is an important document that helps to confirm that Offa was, at this stage, firmly in charge of south-east England. Some of the most interesting aspects of the charter, however, are the exceptions made for things that the churches of Kent were still obliged to finance – in particular, 'an expedition within Kent against seaborne pagans arriving with fleets, or against the East Saxons if necessity compels, as well as bridge and fortress work in Canterbury to see the pagans off'.[3]

Put simply, the Church still had to pay for defences against pagan raids from the sea, and it seems clear from this that Vikings were already threatening the southern shores of Britain in Offa's day. It also follows that there were many incidents of violence, destruction and theft which have left no trace in the written record. That does not necessarily mean that London had been targeted by earlier Viking raids, but it could well have been. The threat, at least, had been alive for more than half a century.

But even if it had suffered no Viking aggression, London would have been no strange port to Scandinavian mariners. Writing in the early eighth century, Bede famously described 'the city of London, which stands on the banks of the Thames, and is a trading centre for many nations who visit it by land and sea'.[4] His thumbnail sketch of a great international emporium is borne out by archaeological evidence found at various places around London's West End suggestive of a thriving trade with the Frankish realms and Frisia via their own respective trading sites at Quentovic and Dorestad.* Some of the imports came from further afield – pottery and quern-stones from the Rhineland, figs from southern Europe – and there may have been direct contact with Ribe in Denmark and, by the eighth century, with new trading ports at Kaupang (Norway), Birka (Sweden) and Hedeby (now in northern Germany).

London's success as a trading centre was bound to the river. From the Rhine estuary, a westward journey pointed straight down the barrel of the Thames. From there the river was a navigable conduit deep into the west of Britain, with the city functioning as the gateway – an entrepôt squatting at the hub of an overland travel network worn into the earth by millennia of falling feet. It was this location that had made London – Londinium – the *de facto* capital of the province of Britannia for most of the first two centuries of Roman rule in Britain.† Roman technology and organization had turned the trackways into an extensive and well-maintained network of roads, connecting the city with the farthest-flung reaches of the province. Over time, Londinium developed the trappings of a great imperial city: a mighty stone basilica, around 560 feet in length

---

* In what are now northern France and the Netherlands respectively.
† In the year 197, when the province of Britannia was divided into two, London's position had been formalized as the capital of the pre-eminent portion (Britannia Superior), with Eboracum (York) at the centre of the northern province (Britannia Inferior). Later, in 293, when the provinces of Britain were further divided, London retained its position as both a provincial capital and the obvious base of operations for the island as a whole.

and three storeys high; a seven-thousand-seat amphitheatre; an elaborate temple to Mithras; an imposing governor's palace complex; a vast circuit of enclosing walls that roughly encompassed the modern City of London, from Aldgate in the west to the Tower in the east, from Moorgate and Barbican in the north to the river in the south, its river wall skirting the edge of the water.

Surviving stretches of Roman wall can still be found in a handful of places, most in the north of the city, imperfectly commemorated in the stretch of road known as London Wall. Turning south onto Noble Street, a stretch of the old masonry can be found submerged in a deep trench, cutting a long rift down the western limb of the road, below the cliffs of glass and steel and pale brick that rise above. The stone is red and raw against the cold sterility of the modern City of London, a livid ridge of muscle exposed where the urban skin has been pulled away by dissecting hands, archaeology as anatomy. A few yards away to the north, a church once stood close to the wall; another wound, this time healed over like a scar, sealed but not forgotten, a sad rectangle of brown brickwork and grass where St Olave Silver Street once stood. First mentioned in the twelfth century, the church was dedicated to a Norwegian warrior-king who died in 1030 – one of several such churches that stud the city.

Like so much of old London, St Olave Silver Street was obliterated by the Great Fire in 1666. Worse was to come, of course. During the 1940s, the war brought unprecedented damage to the body of the city. And what the incendiary bombs failed to claim, the planners and architects of subsequent decades took instead, replacing the surviving fabric with an urban landscape of brutal modernity. Around London Wall the dystopian ramparts of the Barbican Estate rise, grey walkways and balconies, stairwells and underpasses, cold light and hard shadows – a dream of how the future used to look, filtered through the cathode-ray tube and the comic-book pages of *2000AD*: all cyberpunk visions, block-wars and ultraviolence.

It is into this world that the Roman wall runs, its broken towers and bulwarks dwarfed by concrete parapets, corralled into a narrow municipal green space that snakes around the side of the Museum of London. The museum is the final repository for much of the reclaimed detritus of London's many pasts, its Viking Age included. There the recaptured fugitives of lost centuries are confined, trapped uncomfortably by the museum's awkward modernity. Time has dulled the building's once-cutting edge, exposing the built-in obsolescence laid by architectural vanity. The collection is now due to move to the covered market at Smithfield, an elegant and functional space that the self-conscious idiosyncrasies of the Barbican Estate could never have accommodated. It is ironic that, in their flight from failed modernity, the relics of London's past have (one hopes) effected the rescue of the Victorian former meat market from the bulldozer – the General Market Building, designed by the architect Horace Jones and completed in 1883, had at one stage been doomed for demolition and replacement by a seven-storey office block.

* * *

The eeriness of lost pasts and failed futures can be felt everywhere in London. The old, the buried and the mutilated jostle uneasily with the weird, the obsolete and the hyper-modern, leaving the humans that pass in their shadows or tramp over their remains to experience a queer haunting – a nostalgia for the past and for those things that never were, for the futures that were foreclosed or failed to deliver on the promises of their architects; it gives rise to both the city's strange charm and its capacity to unnerve, an arresting ugliness born of a chaotic cycle of trauma, healing and failure, abandonment, recovery and decay. It has been this way since Boudicca massacred the young town's inhabitants and burned it to the ground in the year 60 or 61, and it is, perhaps, the reason why the Anglo-Saxons reacted to London's ruins in the confused ways in which they did – both repelled and fascinated.

For the literate elite, Roman settlements retained an allure of sorts: a memory of former grandeur, of their status as bastions of imperial power and burgeoning Christian hierarchy – suitable settings for the renewal and preservation of faith. At Lincoln, for example, the church of St Paul-in-the-Bail – situated within the old Roman precincts – can be dated to the seventh century, and the town may have retained significance as the seat of a bishop – an oasis of relative civilization amongst the ruins. Things took a similar course within the walls of Londinium, where ideas of *Romanitas* guided the aspirations of bishops, popes and kings. The original church of St Paul's was founded – according to Bede – in 604. It was constructed for Mellitus, its first incumbent bishop, an Italian who had travelled to Britain with Augustine's fateful mission to convert the English to Christianity.[5] Writing to Augustine from Rome, Pope Gregory I had expressed his desire that London should become the primary see of a revived Britannia, the capital of a province restored to the Christian Imperium that he envisaged: an Empire of Christ with Rome at its heart and Britannia at its periphery on the new frontier of Roman Christendom.[6]

Political realities in Britain interfered with Gregory's vision. When Mellitus was eventually installed at London, it was as a bishop subordinate to the archdiocese of Canterbury. The real power in southern Britain was King Æthelberht of Kent (with the apparent acquiescence of his nephew Sæberht, king of Essex). Æthelberht was quite content for his own trading emporium at Canterbury to remain the pre-eminent centre of Roman Christianity in Britain (Augustine himself had been recognized as the first archbishop of Canterbury in 597). Nevertheless, the symbolic importance of London had been recognized, and the church of St Paul's was duly built within the walls. No trace of the original building survives, no indication of its size or grandeur, nor even whether it was raised in stone or timber; but somewhere below the vast hulk of Wren's cathedral, down through the remnants of the great gothic building that burned in 1666, some shattered trace of that Saxon church may yet lie.

Mellitus did not have long to enjoy his episcopal power. When Kings Æthelberht and Sæberht both died in 616–17, the former was replaced by his son Eadbald, and the latter by his own three sons: Sæward, Seaxred and Seaxbald. Unfortunately for Mellitus, all of these men were initially unenthusiastic about the whole idea of Christianity. The sons of Sæberht kicked Bishop Mellitus out of London, and King Eadbald promptly kicked him out of the country. When Eadbald eventually revised his religious opinions and allowed Mellitus to return to Kent in 618–19, the bishop discovered that Kentish royal power had found its limits. Returning to London to resume his ministry, he must have been dismayed to find that its townspeople were not at all pleased to have him back, preferring – as Bede put it – 'their own idolatrous priests'. Faced with the 'refusal and resistance' of London's defiantly pagan townsfolk (backed, we must assume, by the recalcitrant heathen princes of Essex), both Kentish king and Church of Rome were rendered powerless.[7] Armed with enviable geopolitical advantages, the townsfolk did what generations of Londoners have done ever since: they slammed shut the (probably metaphorical) gates and told the bishop to bugger off.*

These anecdotes comprise the earliest written mentions of London in the early Middle Ages, and introduce themes that run throughout the city's history. Poised between kingdoms – Kent and Essex, East Anglia and Mercia, Wessex and, later, the 'Danelaw' – early medieval London was able to routinely exploit the political tensions that ran through and focused on the city. This position at the convergence of frontiers, on the fault lines of effective authority, enabled London to grow prosperous. It could be a meeting place and a bargaining chip, a market place, a hub for intrigue, a centre of international commerce. Its liminality also fostered a sense of independence amongst the city's populace – a belligerence and bloody-mindedness that would,

---

* Shortly afterwards he was made archbishop of Canterbury instead.

over the centuries, manifest itself repeatedly in the teeth of unwelcome demands and unwanted guests. The same attributes, however, would also make the city desirable – an economic and political prize worth any amount of blood and treasure to capture or defend.

That desire for the city – the urge to possess it, to exploit it, to wield authority within and from it – had revealed itself from the beginning as an animating force. It was not, as the story of Mellitus reveals, a desire founded solely in worldly ambitions and practicalities. Of all the former imperial cities of Britannia it was Londinium that Pope Gregory had imagined should form the head of a new Christian province. It was a romantic vision, an image of the Roman Empire reborn as a great commonwealth of faith with Rome at its heart. In that vision, the old cities and provincial capitals would rise from chaos as beacons of religion, learning and orderly government – miniature reflections of the heavenly Jerusalem. This dream of restored empire, fluttering in the breasts of kings and ecclesiarchs, would keep London's weak pulse beating throughout the darkest years of its decay – an image that would sustain it in the minds of those whose deeds would shape its destiny in the years ahead. Two centuries after Mellitus, London remained, in the words of a charter of King Coenwulf of Mercia, 'a famous place and a royal town'.[8]

Yet when those words were written in 811 – and thirty-one years later, when Viking ships sailed past the walls in 842 – the ruins of Londinium had still not been reclaimed. Rotting beside the Thames for more than four centuries, the walls were the relics of a world as far removed from the Viking Age as the Renaissance is from our own. The sight of them may have been something of a novelty for people hailing from lands that had never been yoked to Rome; it might have seemed to them – as it had to the Anglo-Saxons – a ghost town, filled with the shades of fallen empires. The wilful neglect, avoidance even, of the old city of Londinium, indeed of most Roman urban settlements in Britain, is one of the great puzzles of the early Anglo-Saxon period. Some of this reluctance to make use of the old urban environment was no doubt informed by practicality – Londinium's river wall was not very conducive to water-borne trade, and the repair and maintenance of masonry buildings required specialist skills and materials that were hard to acquire. But as a blanket explanation for a widespread phenomenon, this sort of functionalist reasoning feels unduly reductive – and not a little patronizing. Even the rudest of fantasy barbarians could surely find the wherewithal to balance stones one atop the other – or to demolish them when they got in the way.

In truth, the Anglo-Saxons possessed a deep intellectual and emotional sophistication, a clear capacity to make philosophical and aesthetic choices untethered from base economic calculation and utilitarianism. Their imaginative world was rich and complex, their poetry tightly structured yet poignant – sparsely drawn but deeply allusive. Like a bright spring bubbling from the mountain rock, the glittering stream of verse speaks of worlds unseen, of vast caverns and subterranean rivers flowing with forgotten myths and half-remembered pasts.

> Well-wrought this wall-stone, weird broke it;
> Bastions busted, burst is giant's work.

Roofs are ruined, ruptured turrets,
Ring-gate broken, rime on lime-work,
Cloven shower-shields, sheered, fallen,
Age ate under them. Earth-grasp holds fast
The noble workers, decayed, departed
in earth's hard-grip, while a hundred times
the generations pass.[9]

The Ruin, the Old English poem from which the lines above are translated, describes the remains of a Roman city. The poet here has turned the experience of living amongst ruins into an elegiac romanticism weighed down with fate – what the English knew as *wyrd* ('weird') and the Norse as *urðr*; it was a sense, shared amongst the peoples of northern Europe, that all roads led inevitably into darkness – 'that all glory', as Tolkien put it, 'ends in night'.[10]

The environments that played host to these great turnings of the cosmic wheel were therefore not happy places, not conducive to the building of bright futures. The ruin and decay was a reminder of failure and hubris, of the striking hand of fate and the erasures of history, haunted by the workings of time and by the memories of giants. It is for these reasons, as much as for any practical purpose, that the former Roman cities of Britain were shunned. In Londinium, only the small area around St Paul's seems to have remained in use at all, the rest of the city crumbling, filth-strewn and insect-infested. Some of the clearest evidence for a human presence has been found in the shape of two strange corpses, two women of the eighth century whose bodies were disposed of in bizarre circumstances near Bull Wharf, between the river and the walls. The first had died a violent death – her head smashed in with a weapon or a tool, laid on a bed of reeds, covered with moss, enclosed in tree bark, surrounded by wooden stakes. This was not normal. Fifteen feet away another woman lay buried in a narrow grave; a more conventional burial, but still – in its location, its isolation, its association with the weird – a deviation from Anglo-Saxon normality. These corpses speak to us of the ways in which the old city was regarded: as a fitting place for aberration, as a harbour for the dangerous, uncanny dead.

The place that the Vikings had come to pillage in 842 was not the walled Roman city but a new town that had sprung up to the west. Known to the locals as 'Lundenwic', it was an Anglo-Saxon market place of timber homes, workshops and jetties, sprawling along the shoreline of the Thames from what is now the eastern edge of Trafalgar Square to somewhere in the region of St Clement Danes (near Aldwych). It was one of a number of contemporary settlements – including Hamwic (Southampton), Gipeswic (Ipswich) and Eoforwic (York) – that were focused on servicing trade and manufactured goods (the word *wic* is derived from the Latin *vicus*, a settlement that lacked some of the essentials for a true town in the Roman sense). Lundenwic had grown up in the late seventh century to exploit the opportunities afforded by the river and its easy access to the broader waterways of the Channel and beyond, as well as the overland routes and access to the British interior that the Romans had recognized long ago in situating their own city. Lundenwic – to borrow once more from Tolkien – was Lake Town to Londinium's Dale: a wooden market town erected in the long shadow of its shattered stone forebear, awed by the splendour of its predecessor's memory but haunted by its doom.

There are no maps of Lundenwic. There are, in fact, no maps of London at all before the sixteenth century. What we understand of the Anglo-Saxon street plan can only be pieced together from fragmentary mentions of roads and boundaries, from the road-names and the street plan of later periods, and from archaeology. The settlement occupied an area between two Roman roads that ran from east to west – one at the southern edge of the settlement and the other a few hundred yards north of it. They were already centuries old by the time of King Offa (r.757–96). The northern route is still followed by the line of what is now Oxford Street and High Holborn. Originally the Roman road to Silchester, this was a major highway connecting London to the wider countryside and onwards to the kingdom of Wessex. At what is now Marble Arch, this road crossed the Tyburn Brook and met the junction with Watling Street. From Essex in the east all the way to the west Midlands, Watling Street took travellers from Lundenwic to the heart of Offa's Mercia. In the tenth century it was still recognized as a national artery of major military significance – a charter of King Edgar (r.959–75), dated to the beginning of his reign, described it as the *wide here stræt* ('wide army street').[11]

For at least a thousand years, the place we now call Marble Arch – the crossing of Watling Street, the Silchester Road and the Tyburn Brook – has been a potent landmark, a place of communal memory that thrums with ghosts, rough justice and legal assembly. The name of the stream has become synonymous with public hangings: the last execution to take place there (of the highwayman John Austin) was carried out on 3 November 1783. From the Tudor period onward, the gallows was a triple-beamed structure, like a massive wooden version of those odd plastic bits of miniaturized garden furniture one finds in takeaway pizza boxes. Now a strange memorial to the 'Tyburn Tree' stands on a traffic island at the junction of Edgware Road and Bayswater Road: three young oak trees, one for each leg of that morbid timber tripod. As these trees grow, their branches will intertwine, tangling with each other into a weird simulacrum of the awful structure that once loomed in their place; roots feeding on tarmac-sealed death, limbs creaking with swinging ghosts.

For the Anglo-Saxons, the crossroads was the location of the Ossulstone (Oswulf's Stone). This was a mysterious monolith that served as the meeting place of Ossulstone hundred, a regional division of the county of Middlesex that – though it excluded Southwark and the city within the Roman walls – included much of modern London and all of the Anglo-Saxon settlement of Lundenwic. It marked a place under the open sky for the freemen of the hundred to hear the king's laws and pronouncements, to discuss and dispute with their peers, to settle grievances and see justice done. In cases of serious wrongdoing, guilt was often determined by the number (and the status) of the 'oath-helpers' who would swear to the innocence of the accused. Whilst penalties were not always extreme (most cases were settled by the payment of fines that related to the status of the injured party), the most serious and recalcitrant offenders could pay a high price. Hanging and beheading were the most common means of capital punishment, but burning, drowning and stoning – as well as a range of unpleasant mutilations – were also handed down to the unfortunate.

Today the area is dominated by a different monument, the funereal arch of white marble that was moved to the entrance of Hyde Park in 1851. This great rude hunk of architectural salvage from aborted plans for Buckingham Palace stands self-consciously adrift on its traffic island – unsure of its purpose, unmoored from its surroundings, a baroque obsolescence washed up on the flagstone beaches of the mystifying archipelago that (after the arcane traffic schemes of the 1960s) now lies along the chaotic littoral of London's West End. Of the original stone monument – Oswulf's Stone – there is no longer any trace.*

---

* It was apparently still there in 1870, when William Henry Black read an eccentric paper to the London and Middlesex Archaeological Society concerning the apparently regular arrangement of Roman monuments in triangular formations around London. He describes how the stone was buried during the imposition of the new monument but 'is now dug up and lies against the Marble Arch'. Sadly, Black did not choose to describe the stone with the same assiduity with which he elaborated his curious method for locating monumental antiquities. He did, however, note that he had included it amongst his corpus of 'ancient uninscribed stones', and claimed, somewhat misleadingly, that it was noted on John Rocque's map of 1746 as the 'stone where soldiers are shot'. It is not, but a 'Mile Stone' is noted on the map close to the Tyburn gallows. (The place 'where soldiers are shot' is marked opposite the gallows on the north edge of Hyde Park.) One might speculate that Oswulf's Stone had in fact always been a Roman milestone, repurposed and renamed in Old English and used as a landmark and meeting place for Anglo-Saxon worthies and their descendants. Indeed, hundred courts continued to be held there until 1750.[12]

For the people of Lundenwic, however, it was the southern road that held the greater everyday importance during the eighth and early ninth centuries. Connecting the Roman walled city (and the church of St Paul's) with an area of timber-built settlement encompassing what is now Covent Garden and the surrounding environs, the road ran just to the north of the sloping Thames foreshore, overlooking and providing access to the water. Before the twelfth century it was known formally as Akeman Street (*Akemannestraet*), from the Old English name for Bath (*Acemannesceastre*), the Roman city where the road terminated its straight-line drive through the western shires of England.[13] But to the people of Lundenwic, just as to modern Londoners, their local stretch of this great road was almost certainly known by association with the shoreline that it shadowed: the Strand, a word unchanged in sound, form or meaning from the Old English (*strand*: 'shoreline', 'beach', 'bank').[14]

Craven Passage is one of the many crannies that riddle the city behind the grand façades, the modern steel and concrete. These are the mouseholes of history, the places where forgotten vistas and lost walks cling on in the shadows, pattering footsteps and muttered voices caught when the traffic dies away, when the light dims – a stone tape-recording. The Passage, the dingy underbelly of Charing Cross station, is a brick and flagstone vault that bores beneath the platforms of the Victorian station. At its eastern end in the subterranean half-light is the point of egress to Heaven nightclub on Villiers Street, one of the most famous of London's gay clubs. It was just to the south of this dank underpass – part alleyway, part catacomb – that evidence of the Anglo-Saxon embankment was discovered in 1987: to walk the passage from Northumberland Avenue to Villiers Street is to promenade on the edge of Lundenwic's waterfront, to jostle with sailors and dock-hands, barrels and slaves. At its western end the passageway emerges into daylight, splitting The Ship & Shovell into two – the only London pub that occupies both sides of a thoroughfare. Just beyond the pub, the passage crosses Craven Street where, left towards where the water once lapped against the Anglo-Saxon boardwalk, Herman Melville, author of *Moby-Dick*, lived for two months in 1849 at lodgings in number 25 – a handsome end-of-terrace Georgian house that still stands.

The writing of *Moby-Dick* probably began almost at the moment that Melville left London; his journal indicates that he had little enough time for writing amidst visits to the British Museum ('big arm & foot–Rosetta stone–Ninevah sculptures–&c'), antiquarian shopping trips ('Looked over a lot of ancient maps of London. Bought one (A.D. 1766) for 3 & 6 pence'), meetings with publishers and bouts of general indulgence ('Porter passed round in tankards. Round table, potatoes in a napkin. Afterwards, Gin, brandy, whiskey & cigars') – all in all, a fine summation of a writer's ideal life in London. Ideas for the novel, however, were undoubtedly congealing during his stay in the city.[15] 'It is not a piece of fine feminine Spitalfields silk,' wrote Melville in 1851 of his masterpiece, 'but is of the horrible texture of a fabric that should be woven of ships' cables and hausers. A Polar wind blows through it, and birds of prey hover over it.'[16]* It would no doubt have pleased him, thrilled him maybe, to have known that his lodgings were perched above the Anglo-Saxon waterline, where briny-arsed northern sailors once roamed.

The waterfront was further north than it is today, free from the brick and concrete accretions of later centuries that have squeezed the river into an ever-narrowing channel. But even in the eighth century the river's edge was being adapted to human purposes. Fragments of the Anglo-Saxon waterfront have been found near Charing Cross station and Buckingham Street, running from 18–20 York Buildings towards Somerset House, skirting the north edge of Victoria Embankment Gardens. Here the foreshore was embanked with wooden and wattle revetments, creating an artificial timber floor which boats could be brought alongside and goods unloaded on to, and where much of the trade and barter probably took place. This timbered shoreline was the true heart of Lundenwic, a pulsing valve through which people, goods and silver passed back and forth along the water.

Between the Strand and Oxford Street, the other main roads of Lundenwic seem largely to have served as access to and from the waterfront. For the most part these are known from short fragmentary stretches of gravel highway

---

* The same could well be said of most tales of the Viking Age, although we should allow that many a Viking enjoyed the swish of silk on his knees, the fabric imported from the east and sometimes fashioned into voluminous pantaloons. Melville, incidentally, bought himself a pair of pantaloons for one pound five shillings on or near Haymarket on 14 December 1849.[17]

that have been uncovered archaeologically or are inferred from the orientation of buildings. Drury Lane and St Martin's Lane both seem to have been originally laid out in the seventh century as Lundenwic developed, and another north–south route probably ran from Charing Cross to Westminster, and north towards Oxford Street (the Silchester Road). The lines of these roads probably corresponded fairly closely to their modern counterparts, and can be traced in the earliest Tudor maps.

Elsewhere, excavations have produced evidence of narrow gravel lanes, running towards and parallel with the river, lined by rectilinear buildings and ditches laid out in a way that implies a regular street plan: little streets at right angles to each other, the dwellings and workshops of the townspeople set out in tidy rows. At the site of the Royal Opera House, at Maiden Lane and Exeter Street, at 36 King Street and 28–30 James Street and tucked at the north-eastern corner of Covent Garden square itself, the paths and holloways of the Anglo-Saxon settlement carved and crossed, etched into the clay by the footfall of people and beasts, the passage of carts and goods, the flow of games and fights and dancing. Passers-by would have drifted across the fronts of rectangular timber houses, many (though not all) with their gable-ends flush to the roadside, doors opening into rutted filth and stagnant water, mud, gravel and dung. Others were accessed from the long side, from narrow footpaths through yards that stank with refuse and the shit of cows, sheep, pigs, chickens and humans. There were gardens and animals, fences and outhouses, workshops and fruit trees and forges – a humming commu- nity of men, women, children and creatures.

Around a hundred buildings have been discovered in Lundenwic, not all of them active at the same time (many were built on top of the remains of others, making the job of archaeologists harder than it would otherwise be, obscuring and confusing the sequence of habitation at particular locations). The average size of a dwelling or workshop was approximately forty feet long and eighteen feet wide – not palatial by any means, although a cash buyer for that sort of square footage in Covent Garden today would have to be a multi-millionaire. Buildings were timber-framed and single-storey, with walls of wattle and daub and roofs of thatch or oaken shingles; they were heated by rectangular floor-hearths or round ovens, and lit by ceramic oil-lamps and candles. Doors swung on iron hinges and were secured with iron bolts. It was in these buildings – whether homes or workshops or both – that the craftsmen and women of Lundenwic worked.

One of the things that seems to have attracted foreign traders to Lundenwic (and other English *wics*) was worked textile: cloth – both linen and wool – was not merely exchanged at London's market, but was also made there. The evidence can be found across Lundenwic. Finds of spindle whorls and loom weights in considerable numbers imply a substantial output, a craft industry that supplied textiles to serve personal needs and domestic markets as well as to meet a demand for high-quality exports. Particular concentrations of evidence for weaving have been found at two sites that lie on the line of Drury Lane (55–57 Drury Lane and Bruce House at 1 Kemble Street), and at a location in Covent Garden on the edge of Lundenwic, bounded by Shorts Garden, Earlham Street and Neal Street – a stone's throw from Seven Dials.

That Anglo-Saxon cloth was prized on the continent is confirmed by the contents of an extraordinary letter of 796 from Charlemagne (at that time king of the Franks and the Lombards) to King Offa. Evidently, Offa had grumbled about the size of imported quern-stones – used primarily for grinding cereals – as well as some issues concerning the treatment of merchants. Charlemagne responds:

> Now about those black quern-stones you wanted; you had better send a guy over here to tell us what sort of thing you want; then we can sort that out for you and help with the transport. But since you've got into this size issue, I've got to tell you that my guys have a thing or two to say about those short cloaks you've been sending us. You're going to have to get your people to make up some cloaks like they used to, bro; you know – like the ones we used to get back in the day . . . *

Anglo-Saxon cloaks were evidently in demand by the Frankish great and good – the longer, apparently, the better.

It wasn't only weaving that drove the industry of Lundenwic – numerous other crafts were practised in the

---

* The letter was composed in flowery Latin by one of Charlemagne's court servitors – probably the Northumbrian monk Alcuin. One suspects that the great king's true sentiments probably hewed closer to my more colloquial version – and were quite possibly less polite. The original version is, however, peppered with proclamations of brotherly affection.[18]

buildings that once lay between the River Fleet and Tyburn. Antler and bone were turned into combs in workshops where the Royal Opera House extension now stands, quiet work that would have been disturbed by the skriking of hammers from the smithies nearby. Glass was worked and leather was punched, wood was shaped and animals were butchered. What the inhabitants could not produce was brought in from further afield – animal produce from farms outside the settlement, fish caught downriver in the estuary, wine brought from overseas, figs from the Mediterranean, quern-stones from the Rhineland.

All the evidence suggests that Lundenwic in the eighth century was a lively, prosperous place where people lived in relative comfort. They ate bacon and drank ale, munched on apples and warmed their heels by flaming hearths in winter. They crafted day-to-day objects, wove cloth and farmed produce, and presumably took good money and – more often – goods in exchange from the foreign traders who trod the timber embankments beside the Strand. It was a place stocked with humans, young and hale, and animals good for work and food and riding; a place that might well have presented an attractive target to the ruthless and the bold.

Although most of the sailors whose boats arrived at the Strand from overseas would have been Franks or Frisians, it is very likely that Scandinavians were also regular visitors to Lundenwic's markets. Familiarity may well have spurred the raids on Lundenwic and other North Sea emporia

– the Vikings already knew of the wealth to be found in such places, and if they hadn't been there themselves, they had heard about it from others – from friends and kinsmen, from Frisian traders, from chattering monks bound for slavery. Some, perhaps, hawking their wares on the Strand and filling their shallow-keeled ships with good Lundenwic cloth, had made cold calculation even as they bartered: of profits to be made from ships filled with stolen silver, of slaves taken at the sword's edge – the risk of death weighed against the reward of plunder.

If they did, and if the raid of 842 was truly the first of its kind, then they had left it very late to roll the die. By the mid-ninth century, Lundenwic was a shadow of what it had been in the eighth century. Occupation seems to have come to an end in many parts of the settlement, and while activity continued it was no longer as coherent or as wealthy as it had been; it was fragmented, knots of buildings and associated smallholdings scattered over the site of Lundenwic, separated by wasteland and punctuated with rubbish pits. Serious fires had taken a toll – in 764, 798 and 801 – but there should be little doubt that Viking raids were largely responsible for the severe economic malaise that settled in the first half of the ninth century. This is not to say that Lundenwic was no longer important. It was clearly important enough to call down the Viking raid of 842, and a hoard of 250 coins buried around the same time (and possibly related to the Viking threat) stands testament to the wealth that still flowed through the settlement.* Substantial ninth-century ditches, dug at Maiden

---

* Discovered at Middle Temple in what was then open countryside.

Lane and the Royal Opera House, bear witness to both a heightened sense of danger and to the continued presence of something in the region of Covent Garden that was worth labouring to protect. Nevertheless, a lack of security depresses economic growth and investment – as true then as it is now – and the risk to places accessible by water was only growing stronger.

In 851 another Viking fleet entered the Thames. According to the *Anglo-Saxon Chronicle*, 350 ships slid into the estuary, sacking Canterbury before moving on to London. There are no surviving Viking ships that date to the mid-ninth century. The closest parallel to the vessels that attacked London in 851 is a ship recovered from a burial mound at Gokstad near Oslo in Norway. Constructed in the 890s, the Gokstad ship is a beautiful object, a master-piece of technology and design. The strakes of its clinker-built hull taper with the smooth curves of living trees up to the razor-edged prow: a sleek and deadly serpent of the waves. Broad enough in the belly for a substantial crew and cargo, but still fast and lethal under sail and oar, the Gokstad ship could have carried around thirty-five rowers, all of whom would probably have been expected to fight. If ships of the fleet that entered the Thames in 851 were of similar size, and if the numbers provided by the *Chronicle* are accurate, this Viking warband could have fielded up to 12,250 warriors.

This is a large number by any measure, and the reported size of Viking fleets and armies has been repeatedly called into question over the years, with suspicions that the numbers were inflated by monastic writers to heighten the sense of existential danger and to excuse Anglo-Saxon defeats. Nevertheless, it is likely that this was a serious threat. From the 850s onward, the nature of the Viking threat to the Anglo-Saxon kingdoms had changed. Large forces, bigger than those that had raided the coastline of Britain in previous decades, began to 'over-winter' – that is, to set up camp rather than go home over the off-season, maintaining a pattern of raiding and mounting ever more damaging and ambitious campaigns. The raid on London in 851 was effectively the dawn of this grim new day: it is recorded in the same *Chronicle* entry that 'for the first time, heathen men settled over the winter'.[19] It also marked the effective end of Lundenwic, both in reality – within a couple of decades the settlement had become archaeologically invisible, covered by a layer of dark earth – and in the minds of near-contemporaries.* According to the retrospective account in the *Anglo-Saxon Chronicle*, written in the 890s, the attack of 851 was launched not against Lundenwic, but against *Lundenburh*: against 'fortress London'.

---

* A hoard of Northumbrian coins (known as 'stycas'; see page 45), discovered in excavations at the Royal Opera House, was buried around 851; their deposition may well be associated with the Viking raid of that year.

II

Lundenburh

I
n 865, a *micel hæðen here* (a 'great heathen horde')
arrived in East Anglia. It was a Viking warband larger
than any seen before in Britain, and with extraordinary
speed it set about tearing up the geopolitical order, shat-
tering ancient kingdoms the length and breadth of the
island: Northumbria (866), East Anglia (870), Alt Clud
(870), Mercia (873) – all fell to the conquerors or were
transformed out of all recognition. In England, only Wessex
remained intact, preserved by good fortune and the fortitude of its rulers.

In 871, returning from Wessex after having been fought
to a standstill by Alfred and his brother, King Æthelred,
the great heathen horde had made camp at London and
remained there over the winter. A hoard of silver found at
Croydon can be dated to this period, and may well relate
to the comings and goings of Viking warbands from their
winter-setl at London. The Mercian King Burgred

eventually 'made peace' with the Viking army (i.e. paid them off), and they returned to East Anglia. It was to be a short-lived reprieve – the Vikings invaded Mercia in 873, deposing Burgred and driving him into exile. In 878 a different Viking fleet, lately arrived from the continent, made camp at Fulham – then a site to the west of London. It too left after a single winter, travelling to Ghent (in modern Belgium) before rampaging onward into the Frankish kingdom.

There is no record that details activity at either of these camps, and no archaeology to pinpoint their locations or illuminate the day-to-day lives of their temporary inhabitants. 'It is very difficult,' as one historian has put it, 'to gather from these random comings, goings and hibernations any coherent impression of what the occupation amounted to.'[1] The circumstances may have varied. The earlier camp might have been either within or without the walls of the city; either around the precincts of St Paul's or thrown up west of the Fleet River amongst the derelict remains of Lundenwic. The camp at Fulham was perhaps more likely to have been newly built, a freshly laid out site with access to the Thames. Excavated Viking camps at Torksey (Lincolnshire), Repton (Derbyshire) and another site in North Yorkshire suggest that such camps covered extensive areas and hummed with activity. Trade, manufacture, engineering, gaming and family life – the site at Torksey has revealed all of this on a site of over sixty-five acres, more a small town than a temporary barracks.

Whatever conditions were like inside the perimeter of the camps at London and Fulham, relations with the locals were likely tense and probably violent. Raiders plundering the local countryside would have first secured the winter essentials – pigs, cattle, grain, ale – before coming for the horses, the silver, the women. It was a burden felt widely. The bishop of Worcester, Wærferth, was forced to sell off some of his land to cope with the 'very pressing affliction and immense tribute of the barbarians, in that same year when the pagans stayed in London'.[2] Neither camp seems to have lasted more than a season, and the immediate threat of Viking occupation was in both cases transient. But in the fields and farms beyond the city, the world was changing fast, old certainties falling away sharply. In a little over a decade from the advent of the great horde in 865, two of the kingdoms that had traditionally exerted influence over London had been conquered (East Anglia) or dismantled (Mercia) by Viking armies. And although Alfred's Wessex had endured, the resulting peace had left London on the front line of a volatile border. The story of how Alfred defeated an army led by the Viking leader Guthrum at Edington (Wiltshire) in 878, of how he had dwelt in the fen-fastness of Athelney (Somerset) before returning to smite his enemies like the avenging sword of the Almighty, has been told many times. Like all of the literary products of its time and place, it is replete with Alfredian myth-making.

In the peace that followed Edington (and the so-called Treaty of Wedmore), Alfred extracted from his erstwhile foe a number of key concessions, including his baptism and an agreement to change his name from Guthrum to Æthelstan. The key part of the whole ritualized encounter seems to have been – from Alfred's perspective at least – the acceptance by Guthrum-Æthelstan of a symbolic filial subordination: he became, in the process of baptism, Alfred's godson. It was a tacit acceptance of Alfred's over-lordship – an agreement to be his man. And though it might seem from a West Saxon perspective like total victory – a heathen warrior humbled, forced to his knees to kiss the cross and the ring of his conqueror – in reality it is hard to believe that Guthrum received nothing in return, that his defeat had been so total that it warranted nothing but humiliation.

Instead it seems likely that the negotiations included the recognition of Guthrum-Æthelstan as king of East Anglia – albeit a king who owed notional fealty to Alfred as his 'father' and overlord. Certainly, when the two men next met, it was perceived as a royal summit: the so-called Treaty of Alfred and Guthrum styles both men as 'rex'. Amongst other provisions, that treaty – which is broadly datable to somewhere between 878 and Guthrum's death in 890 – defined the respective spheres of influence of both kings. The dividing line was to be a boundary that ran 'up the Thames, and then up the Lea, and along the Lea to its source, then in a straight line to Bedford, then up the Ouse to Watling Street'. It was a treaty which conspic-uously, and with obvious deliberation, scored a boundary around London, keeping it tucked just within the limits of Alfred's authority.

Today the River Lea empties out into the Thames in Poplar, just east of the Isle of Dogs. To walk its course upriver is to pass through Stratford and past Hackney Marshes to Tottenham, Edmonton, Walthamstow, the river filling the Lea Valley reservoir chain, Epping Forest stretching away to the east. Its path carves through the

Olympic Park, the 'Olympicopolis' so despised by Iain Sinclair: a 'city of pop-ups, naming rights, committee-bodged artworks, cash-cow academies, post-truth blogs and charity runs', an 'emerging digital conceit on the Viking bank of the River Lea'.[3] Sinclair seems at times unmoored by despair, enraged by the changes wrought by corporate money and empty technocracy on the cherished, untidy banks of the river. During construction of the Olympic Park he beat like an angry wasp against the notorious blue fence that enclosed the development, body and rhetoric levelled against the barrier. After Olympicopolis inevitably shimmered into three dimensions, he railed at this 'theme park still to identify its theme', still 'waiting on input from a content provider'.[4]

Alfred, I am sure, would have approved of the Olympic Park; he emerges from the sources as a lover of order, a man didactic in his inclinations, managerial in style. He admired the Romans, planned grand building projects, enjoyed a good right-angle. I imagine he would have agreed that clean-liness is next to godliness. The world he and his scribes envisaged was a place of order and easy management, of binary choices and simple ethnicities: English, Danish; Christian, Heathen; Good, Bad. There were no shades of grey in Alfred's little England, no room for conflicted loyal-ties, identities or beliefs: those things were chaos, and chaos lived beyond the pale in *fifelcynnes eard* – in 'monster world'.[5] In the ninth century, it was the slow drift of the Lea that became the *limes*, the tear in the fabric that separated Alfred's 'Anglo-Saxon' realm from another place – a world of confused allegiances and sundered bonds, where the alien Guthrum reigned as king of East Anglia and a host of unnamed Viking warlords and embattled Anglo-Saxon thegns struggled to make sense of a disordered world.

In truth, it is hard to imagine how this boundary was ever inscribed in reality – there were no ramparts, no watchtowers. No wall. Even within the city, the lines of authority were blurred, a messy West Saxon/Mercian compromise involving Kentish and Mercian bishops and the shadow of the new Scandinavian regime in East Anglia.* As a notional approximation of the length of Alfred's reach, the treaty placed London at the very tips of his outstretched fingers, barely within his grasp.

Perhaps it was this sense of insecurity that informed the tenor of what is perhaps the most famous of all mentions of London to emerge from the *Anglo-Saxon Chronicle*, the record of a moment that has taken on an almost mythic status in the history of the city and of the nation, the moment in 886 when 'King Alfred restored [*gesette*] fortress London [*Lundenburh*], and all the English [*Angelcyn*] turned to him, except for those in bondage [*hæftniede*] to Danish men [*Deniscra manna*], and he then bestowed [*befæste*] the stronghold on Ealdorman Æthelred to hold'.[7] This, the *Chronicle* wishes us to know, is a moment for the ages, the apotheosis of English kingship, the reclaiming of London's imperial destiny, the moment when Alfred transcended West Saxon parochialism to lay claim to a greater inheritance: a new realm, a realm of all the English, united against the

---

* A charter drawn up at a meeting to discuss the 'the renewal of the city of London' involving the bishops of Winchester and Worcester, Ealdorman Æthelred and his wife Æthelflæd, and King Alfred.[6]

common foe. Alfred had come to London as defender and liberator, to restore and to build, to fortify the mighty stronghold-city on the borders of his kingdom, to renew the legacy of Rome.

And yet, to turn a critical eye to the words and phrases the scribe employs in this one sentence is to find the half-truths, omissions and over-simplifications falling over themselves.

According to the mighty dictionary of Old English originally compiled by John Bosworth in 1838 and added to in 1898 and 1921 by Thomas Northcote Toller, the verb *gesettan* has numerous meanings – sixteen, in fact: 'to set, put, fix, confirm, restore, appoint, decree, settle, possess, occupy, place together, compose, make, compare, expose, allay'.* Thus, one could say that Alfred 'restored' London; or that he 'settled' it; or that he 'occupied' it. Indeed, from this multiplicity of meanings an elaborate narrative could be constructed: of Alfred capturing the city, restoring its defences, settling it with new inhabitants, issuing it with new laws and status, publicly affirming its place as an important and indissoluble bastion of the new English realm. On the other hand, it need not mean any more than that the king had some sort of formal triumph to confirm his status, or, even more weakly, that he simply wished to announce his 'possession' of London in some abstract and remote sense. If so, this might have amounted to little more than a putting-into-writing of a *de facto* situation that may

---

* This list ignores the variety of ways that the verb *settan* (without its perfective prefix *ge-*) can be read, along with its myriad other compound forms.[8]

have already been recognized for some time. By the same token, it could have signified the implementation of some entirely novel political arrangement.

This ambiguity was probably deliberate. In reality, Alfred had no traditional claim to London at all: the city had been part of the Mercian kingdom since the seventh century. It is true that West Saxon influence there had been on the increase. Earlier in the ninth century, in 829, London-based moneyers had briefly produced coins for the West Saxon King Ecgberht after his military suppression of Mercia in that year; and Alfred's power and authority had been apparent in London from the 870s onward, with London moneyers producing coins in his name alongside those of the Mercian kings Burgred and Ceolwulf. But the city had never been convincingly absorbed by the West Saxon realm. In fact, the man upon whom the *Chronicle* claims Alfred 'bestowed the stronghold' – 'Ealdorman' Æthelred – was probably (or had been) the king of Mercia, at least in his own mind and sometimes in the minds of his own people and his enemies.[9] For many people London was therefore already Æthelred's patrimony – not Alfred's to bestow.

Nor is there any real evidence to suggest that London was ever in thrall to Viking power during the ninth century, no Danish yoke for Alfred to manfully lift from the necks of the oppressed *Angelcyn*. The only indication of Viking occupation (besides the 886 *Chronicle* entry) is a retrospectively inserted reference to a siege of 883 – when Alfred's army was 'encamped against the horde at London'.[10] If this event did in fact properly occur in 883 (which is not universally accepted), it is utterly without context: any number of scenarios involving West Saxons, Vikings and Mercians (as well as the Londoners themselves) could be conjured to explain it. It could even be that this siege was intended to consolidate Alfred's authority over the city and to force Æthelred to recognize his demotion in the Anglo-Saxon pecking order. (The earliest evidence for Æthelred's acceptance of Alfred's overlordship comes from a charter dated to 883, the same year as the siege.) The events of 886, therefore, might in fact describe a carefully choreo-graphed diplomatic entente between the two rulers – a mutual face-saving affair at which Alfred's over-kingship was affirmed, but Æthelred's practical lordship acknow-ledged. If this were the case, it would explain why the siege of 883 was excluded from the official West Saxon record: an inconclusive attempt to bully Mercian London sat awkwardly with Alfred's later concern with promoting the image of himself as saviour and liberator of all the English, Mercian Angle and West Saxon alike.

In any case, regardless of technical authority, London had long been a place where a multitude of regional iden-tities collided and merged. Here the people of Kent and Essex, East Anglia and Mercia, Surrey and Wessex butted snugly up against one another to meet and trade and mingle, not to mention the Britons, Northumbrians, Frisians, Franks and Scandinavians who came as visitors, traders and settlers, forging long-term relationships with the place and its people. It is more than likely that the city's inhabitants, if they did not identify with their own regional origins, thought of themselves primarily as Londoners (Anglo-Saxon sources refer to the inhabitants as *burgware* or *Lunden-ware*: literally 'stronghold-dwellers' or 'London-dwellers'). Any notion of Englishness, of *Angel*-kinship, came much later.

Nevertheless, in the long term the popularization of an inclusive sense of 'Englishness' was a triumph of Alfredian propaganda. The concept of a single English community had never had a clear limit to its compass beyond a vague sense of linguistic community and some tenuous notions of overseas origins. Before Alfred's regime got hold of them, even these ideas may not have spread far beyond the ecclesiastic think-tanks in which they were spawned. The idea of Englishness preceded the reality, logos before demos. It was as a result of the king's programme of education, translation, literary commission and propaganda that the *Angelcyn* were transformed into a people, a *gens*, a *folc*. The English, united by language and faith, were provided with a name and a shared heritage – the latter assiduously constructed in the pages of the *Anglo-Saxon Chronicle* and elsewhere. At the outset, the very flimsiness of the concept was its genius; a semiotic sleight-of-hand that collapsed the regional and ethnic identities of any English-speakers who drifted within its capacious and ill-defined orbit into a singularity, both infinite and void.

What Englishness truly depended on, however, was its negative. To be English was to not be Welsh (*wealas*; 'foreign'), a longstanding distinction to be found in the earliest English law-codes. But crucially for the new *Angelcyn* of Alfred's day, it really crystallized in not being *denisc* ('Danish'). What exactly the term '*denisc*' signified is equally vexed. It didn't mean 'Danish' in any simple sense of national or geographical origin. At the most basic level it seems to have applied to people who spoke in the 'Danish tongue' – i.e. anyone who spoke a Scandinavian language. But it came to be used as a catch-all for the various foreigners and malefactors from whom the *Angelcyn* needed – according to West Saxon writers – to be rescued. And it is here that the purpose of this Alfredian ethnogenesis reveals itself.

Over the course of the following century, Alfred and his descendants would eventually conquer and consolidate their power over all of what is now England and beyond. With pretensions to sweeping overlordship in Britain, the claim to be natural rulers of a people so vaguely and expansively defined as the *Angelcyn* gave to Alfred and his descendants the imagined right to rule over an equally vague and expansive realm. Moreover, the creation of two simple oppositional categories – white hats vs. black hats, *Angelcyn* vs. *Deniscra manna* – provided the ubiquitous enemies that violent ambitions demanded. The 'Dane' could be a bad-guy for all seasons, a bogeyman to justify territorial usurpation, the suppression of independent rule from the Thames to the Tees. Every act of aggression could be sold as reconquest or liberation, every new subject an Englishman, every slain enemy a Dane. England was to be a boundless nation, as elastic as the capabilities and ambitions of its rulers.

And so it is worth reflecting on the *Chronicle* entry for 886, to consider how effective and how subtle Alfredian propaganda could be. In the space of a single short sentence, the chronicler had made a henchman of a royal peer and a chattel of his patrimony, had raised a dilapidated church precinct to a fortified metropolis, had wrung foundational myth from political expediency, had discovered an English folk-hero in a ruthless political dynast: Alfred the builder, Alfred the liberator, Alfred the great.

Lundenburh: even the name the *Anglo-Saxon Chronicle* had started to apply was a loaded one.[11] The use of the word *burh* or *byrig* to describe Anglo-Saxon settlements was not entirely new in the ninth century – it had been used in much earlier place-names to describe Iron Age hill-forts and other defensible places – but came to be associated with new developments in urban planning that have long been attributed to Alfred, his son Edward and his daughter Æthelflaed in their efforts to resist, contain and later roll back Viking domination of much of northern and eastern England. Most famously, a number of burhs were listed in a document known to historians as the *Burghal Hidage*, an assessment of the manpower required to man and maintain the defences of a West Saxon network of fortified places that ranged from new-built settlements to revived hill-forts and Roman walled towns. These places would become significant not only militarily as garrisons and secure depots, but also as secure locations for trade and aspects of administration: mints were frequently situated at burhs in the later Anglo-Saxon period. So, although they may not have been conceived of primarily as towns, they swiftly – and sometimes permanently – took on many of the urban functions and characteristics that had previously been split between emporia and other types of royal and monastic estate centres.

Although London itself was not one of the settlements listed in the *Burghal Hidage*, as a strategically, economically and symbolically important town it certainly sat comfortably alongside other walled Roman towns that received attention around the same time (e.g. Exeter, Winchester, Bath). The sort of investment that settlements new and old were receiving in the latter decades of the ninth century can be discerned in Bishop Asser of Sherborne's contemporary biography of Alfred. He describes how the king ordered 'cities and towns to be rebuilt [and] others to be constructed where previously there were none [. . .] royal halls and chambers marvellously constructed of stone and wood [. . .] royal residences of masonry, moved from their old position and splendidly reconstructed at more appropriate places by his royal command'.[12]

The image that Asser initially presents is of a nation furiously engaged in major building projects, labouring like termites to raise a new Jerusalem of gleaming stone, groaning with 'treasures incomparably fashioned in gold and silver'.[13] In truth, even Asser could not disguise the reluctance of Alfred's subjects to give themselves wholeheartedly over to these prodigious labours, noting that the king was given to 'sharply chastising those who were disobedient' and, with unbending schadenfreude, remarking that those who lost their homes, possessions and loved ones to Viking raids had been taught a well-deserved lesson for having 'negligently scorned the royal commands [. . .] with respect to constructing fortresses and to the other things of general advantage to the whole kingdom'.[14]

This evident disinclination towards onerous labour should be a reminder that, however he saw himself and wished others to see him, Alfred did not speak with the voice of Ramesses. Kings in the early medieval period had very practical limits to their authority: their ability to get things done depended on complex relationships with land-holders and the Church, with intangible qualities of legitimacy derived from their actions and ancestry, from religious sanction and the limits of forceful coercion, from the mundane workings of taxation and communication. Just because the king wanted his palaces 'moved from their old position and splendidly reconstructed at more appro-priate places' didn't necessarily mean that this was going to happen when the king wanted it done – or at all.

In fact, the archaeology of London within the walls for the period of the so-called Alfredian restoration is very limited. Whatever London was to become over the century ahead, in 886 it was little more than it had been in the century prior: in large part a sprawling, weed-choked ruin, with a small-scale development clustered around the church that endured near its western wall. Nevertheless, the direction of travel had been set. Whatever intention lay behind Alfred's public gestures and postures, by the 880s the Londoners had determined that their future lay within the walls, that security trumped flexibility, and that whatever ghosts had originally kept them from the Roman city looked likely to make better neighbours than Vikings. By the mid-ninth century, large areas of the old settlement of Lundenwic had already been abandoned. The bustling nucleus of the late eighth century had fragmented, with smaller areas of occupation at the Royal Opera House and St Martin-in-the-Fields. None of this would survive the ninth century, the streets and houses of the Strand and Drury Lane rotting back into the soil, the wattled embank-ments drowned in river mud.

New investment within the walls had got off to a slow start, but actually seems to have predated Alfred's interest in the city – impelled perhaps by the raids and fires that afflicted Lundenwic from the mid-ninth century. In 857, Ealhhun, bishop of Worcester, was granted an estate known as *Ceolmundingchaga*, 'the estate of the Ceolmundings' (the descendants of Ceolmund).[15] It was located 'not far from the west gates' – probably somewhere in the vicinity of Ludgate and Newgate. Meanwhile, down at the waterfront, commercial interests were beginning to take hold, new markets opening up at breaches in the old Roman river wall. One excavated site – at Bull Wharf in the west of the city – has revealed a long sequence of development and commercial activity. The earliest datable artefacts found there are two Northumbrian stycas, the unprepossessing copper coins of the most northerly Anglo-Saxon realm. These can be dated fairly closely (c.840–c.850 and c.843–c.855), and cannot therefore have been lost before around 840. They were joined by three half-pennies minted for Alfred in c.880, each bearing a distinctive design on the reverse: the Latin form of the city's name – LVNDONIA – rendered down to an elegant monogram.

Alfred's efforts to demonstrate his claims to lordship were sometimes heavy-handed, bordering on crass. The ostentatious London monogram coinage of the 880s – heavy coins with a high silver content – were a precocious triumph of graphic design. The other side, the obverse, bore the name of the king and his image in the guise of a Roman emperor. It was, in its totality, a masterpiece of ideological advertising; a coin which, caught spinning in the sun, conflated city with Caesar, power and place. Other kings before Alfred had advertised the origins of their coins – none more famously than the celebrated Coenwulf mancus, a stunning and so far unique gold coin found in Bedfordshire in 2001 and purchased by the British Museum for £357,832 in 2006. That coin includes the circumscription 'DE VICO LVNDONIAE' – 'from Lundenwic' – surrounding an eight-petalled mandala. But none before Alfred had turned the name of the city into a sigil – a mark of power that overwhelmed even the cross that floated above it.[*]

---

[*] Civic monograms were not in themselves an innovation. In England, a mint monogram for Canterbury had appeared on coins from the early ninth century onward.

Bull Wharf is gone now, disembowelled by archaeologists and obliterated by nondescript glass and steel; a nameless aquarium for bankers. Follow a path beside its western flank toward the Thames, however, and there the old river's shoreline lies bare for a hundred feet or so – a scrape of shingle in the redeveloped embankment. This is Queenhithe, its name part-derived from the Old English word for port (*hyþ*: 'hithe'). It is no more than a grubby cove where the murky water laps at the piles holding the city up above the flood: stones the colour of rusting iron, putrid grey sludge, venom-green riverweed. There were teenagers sitting on the dirty beach the day I walked down to Queenhithe: pouting selfies against the slime and concrete; crushed cans of Tyskie and Monster Energy; small change and condoms; Marlboro packets. None of it very different really from the shite that mudlarks dig from the river every day: copper coins, clay pipes, bits of pottery, broken glass. The rubbish of the Viking Age is made more precious simply by its rarity and the fact that only the most robust detritus has made it through the last millennium. The name has changed: in Alfred's day it was known as Æthelred's hithe (*Ætheredeshythe*), in recognition of the lord of the Mercians who ran the city. That history has been effectively erased. The modern wall that runs beside the hithe now displays 'The Alfred Plaque', a dismal notice 'erected in 1986 to mark the eleven hundredth anniversary of King Alfred's resettlement of the Roman City of London in 886': the depressing triumph of blowhard propaganda.

Æthelred's hithe is referred to (the first time only indirectly) in charters of 889 and 898–9 – documents that detail grants of land that lay unequivocally within the bounds of the city walls.[16] The earlier of these charters is a grant to the bishop of Worcester of a precisely measured plot of land, bounded by the city wall (*murus civitatis*) and a public road (*strata publica*). The plot was defined by an 'ancient stone building' known as 'Hwætmund's stone', and from here, and from the 'trading shore' (*ripa emptoralis*) and the street nearby, the bishop derived tolls on commerce. No one knows for sure what Hwætmund's stone was, but it is likely that this was an Old English name long ago bestowed on Roman ruins that still stood near the river wall – the broken shell, perhaps, of some lost public building, a once-grand civic space whose shattered remnants now provided the bounds of a market place, bustling with the goods and travellers who came there from road and river. The second charter, from around ten years later, describes two plots of land that were both situated at Æthelred's hithe. One, the eastern plot, was granted to the bishop of Worcester, and it is likely that it describes (and reconfirms) the grant of 889. The other plot was granted to the archbishop of Canterbury. The two plots were separated by a road running between them, and both were bounded to the north by another thoroughfare and to the south by the city wall. Beyond that, the bishops had the right to moor their ships on the river.

Understanding how the city plan developed in these early years of renewal is a challenge – an exercise in corre-lating scraps of archaeology, the clues left in land charters, the shape of the city in later medieval maps, the evidence of place names. To the east of London Bridge, archaeolog-ical traces of buildings and road surfaces at Fish Street Hill and Botolph Lane suggest late-ninth-century origins for the streets running south from Cheapside, the old Roman road that ran towards Newgate past the cathedral church of St Paul's. Remains at Bow Lane likewise suggest a late-ninth-century origin for this road and for Garlick Hill to the south, a single street sprouting laterally towards the river from Cheapside. Over to the west, the medieval streets of Little Trinity Lane and Bread Street formed the eastern and western boundaries of the bishop of Worcester's land. Bread Street separated the Worcester and Canterbury plots: it is still there to be walked, though it no longer reaches Upper Thames Street where the old waterfront once lay. Bread Street now sputters out at the nineteenth-century sweep of Queen Victoria Street, and the area to the south is a mess of modern development. But the shape of the bishop of Worcester's land is still just discernible, bounded to the west by the surviving scrap of Little Trinity Lane, and to the east by the outer edges of Cleary Garden.

Elsewhere along the riverbank, place-names ending in *hyþ* – most of them long-forgotten – suggest the places where ships drew up at the dawn of the city's revival: east of Queenhithe, Garlickhithe lay at the foot of Garlick Hill; Timberhithe, to the immediate west of Queenhithe, is now High Timber Street, an obsolete lane that disappears into a striplit underpass, a concrete hellmouth into the urban void. Turning left towards the river, into Broken Wharf, a cheerless service road (Trig Lane) is where boats once moored at Fishhithe.* And from somewhere behind it all comes the whip-crack of sail rope, the stink of tar and fish oil.

---

* As with Queenhithe, the first elements in all of these place-names probably post-date the Viking Age, but *hyþ* is an indisputably old word.

Around the end of the ninth century, the evidence from Bull Wharf begins to thicken. Timber walkways were constructed, gangplanks to ease passage from river to strand. The finds also increase in number, the dates of their disposal approximate, but spanning the latter parts of the ninth century and the earlier parts of the tenth. They make an extraordinary ensemble: a collection of brooches, mounts and other oddments, nearly all of foreign craftsmanship. Many of them are Frankish and Frisian, disc brooches and pseudo-coin brooches and narrow brooches shaped like creeping caterpillars, testament to a burgeoning relationship with Britain's closest overseas markets. But amongst them are finds of Viking craft: a rare copper brooch of a type known to have been manufactured at Hedeby (near modern Schleswig), a buckle with the characteristic punch-marked decoration of the Norse colonies of the Irish Sea, pieces from combs of Scandinavian workmanship, components from a balance scale – the indispensable apparatus of Viking Age commerce. As a group, these finds make up the largest collection of Scandinavian artefacts in Britain after those found at York.

At the beginning of *Moby-Dick*, Melville provided a compendium of cetological miscellanea, 'higgledy-piggledy whale statements' that the author described as a 'glancing bird's eye view of what has been promiscuously said, thought, fancied, and sung of Leviathan, by many nations and generations, including our own'.[17] The ninth of these nuggets of whale-lore – the first that is neither biblical nor classical – is an extract from a narrative written down in Wessex in the late ninth century at the court of King Alfred. It is written in the third person, but captures the testimony of a visitor from the far north who, thanks to the vagaries of the historical record, must stand for any and all such individuals who passed through Anglo-Saxon lands in those days. His name was Ohthere, and he came bearing whale teeth (walrus tusks) as a gift for the king. He told Alfred 'that he, of all the Norwegians, lived the north-most', in Hålogaland, and explained how his days were taken up with whale hunting, reindeer herding and tribute gathering.[18] He also described his southern journeys by sea to the tip of Norway and on to the trading town of Hedeby. There he would mingle and, presumably, do business with the Wends, Saxons and Angles who frequented the place.*

No one can know for certain how much direct trade there was between London, Scandinavia and the Viking-settled parts of Britain, or exactly how many Viking traders could be regularly found hawking their goods at London markets. But the archaeology from Bull Wharf, and the evidence of contact with men like Ohthere and their wider trading networks, suggests that, by the time of Alfred's death in 899, the Scandinavian world was already lapping at the Thames foreshore and spilling into London streets.

* * *

---

* 'Saxons' and 'Angles' here refers to ethnic groups inhabiting what is now northern Germany and southern Denmark. The Wends were a people who inhabited the southern shores of the Baltic Sea east of the Jutland peninsula.

The *Anglo-Saxon Chronicle* has little to say of what went on inside the walls of London as the ninth century closed out. What it does make clear, however, is that the burgeoning fortress city and its garrison remained on the front line.

In 892, a Viking warlord named Hæsten brought eighty ships into the mouth of the Thames. He stopped short of approaching the city itself, however, ultimately tracking south into the River Swale and building a stronghold at Milton Regis in Kent. His was the second fleet to arrive in Britain that year – 250 ships had already turned up at Lympne on the south Kentish coast. A third Viking army arrived from the continent at the same time, making camp at Appledore in Devon. These groups were soon joined by bands of Vikings who had earlier settled in East Anglia and Northumbria. These events presented a serious challenge to Alfred's rule – even to the survival of his realm. They also demonstrated the wisdom of his earlier political instincts. Guthrum-Æthelstan had died in 890, and the impression given by subsequent events is that his death was a liberating event for hungry predators – a heel lifted from the throat of the wolf, any restraint that the late king's Wessex-backed authority had imposed evaporating with his demise. 'As often as the other hordes went out in all their power,' the *Anglo-Saxon Chronicle* explains, the East Anglians 'either went along with them or alone of their own accord.'[19] The various jarls and warbands settled within the notional bounds of the kingdom were free to act as they wished, and no one was left in the east to contain other Vikings arriving from Northumbria and overseas.

Happily for Alfred's subjects, the imposition of burh-building and other military obligations was paying dividends. In 893 a portion of Alfred's army, moving east-ward (while the rest of the army was occupied in the west), arrived at London. There they were joined by the city's garrison and waited for further reinforcements before heading east, across the Lea, on into Essex. Their target was a fortress at Benfleet that had earlier been constructed by Hæsten and occupied by a portion of his army. The English army seems to have caught the Vikings unpre-pared: 'they put that horde to flight, broke down the stronghold, and seized all that was inside it, both money and women and also children, and brought all into London; and all the ships they either broke up or burned or brought to London town or to Rochester'.[20] (Hæsten, however, had gone out on a raid, so lived to fight another day.)

The use of London as a staging post and source of manpower for offensive raids outside English territory prefigured the way that burhs came to be employed by Alfred's son and grandson over the course of the following thirty years. In much the same way that castles were employed by Norman conquerors in the eleventh century, burhs would become forward positions in the creeping West Saxon conquests that led ultimately to a unified kingdom of England. It wasn't always an unqualified success. In 895, the London garrison (with some rein-forcements from elsewhere) attempted to dislodge a Viking war fleet that had used the Lea itself, cutting north from the Thames and building a stronghold twenty miles north of London (somewhere near Hertford). At first it went badly: '[the English] were put to flight there, and some four king's thegns killed'. It took Alfred himself arriving with reinforcements to dislodge the raiding army, blockading the river with new fortifications to prevent the Vikings from making use of their ships. Trapped at Hertford they fled westwards overland, 'and the men of London fetched the ships, and all that they could not take away, broke up, and those that were serviceable brought into London'.[21]

Alfred died in 899 and was succeeded by his son Edward. As the tenth century opened, the Viking wars were moving ever further from London. West Saxon and Mercian armies pressed north and east, plunging deeper into the Viking-dominated parts of Britain – eastern Mercia, Northumbria, East Anglia. When in 910 Æthelred, lord of the Mercians, died, Edward claimed London and Oxford ('and all the lands that pertained thereto'). It was essentially a land grab, a means to choke Mercia's already crippled independence. Although Æthelred's wife, Alfred's daughter Æthelflæd, ruled most of Mercia independently for the next seven years, when she died in 917 her daughter Ælfwynn was forcibly deposed as lady of the Mercians. Edward made himself king of all Mercia, and every English king of the West Saxon dynasty thereafter claimed it as patrimony. It was the end of Mercia as a distinct realm.

Edward's campaigns in the east, though presented as a 'reconquest' – the liberation of Anglo-Saxon people from the tyranny of the Danes – ultimately did the same for East Anglia, ending its independence more thoroughly than the Vikings had ever managed.

In 912 Edward had built new strongholds at Hertford and Witham (Essex). The chronicler's perspective in the matter is clear when he writes that 'a good part of the people who were earlier under the control of Danish men submitted to him'.[22] How happy they were about the change in management is left unsaid, but it is clear that local people were becoming increasingly capable of looking after their own interests: in 913, the formidable folk of Luton on the River Lea caught up with a band of Viking raiders, 'reduced them to full flight and rescued all that they had captured and also [took from them] a great part of their horses and their weapons'.[23] In 916, Edward built a fortress at Maldon (Essex) and subdued Bedfordshire. The following year, his armies captured Colchester (Essex), and – after fortress work at Huntingdon – received the submission of all Essex and East Anglia and the surrender of the Viking army at Cambridge. By 917, after seven breathless years, the boundary of Alfred and Guthrum had been rendered utterly meaningless. For the inhabitants of southern Britain, the Viking Age had been placed on hold.

In 980, when a Viking fleet raided Thanet, there would have been few living in southern England whose prior experience of Scandinavian mariners was violent. For many, the threat of Viking raids had become a distant memory, a tale told in childhood by the veterans of Alfred's wars. The last documented Viking assault had been an attack on Sussex in 894, put to flight by the Chichester garrison; since then, no conflict of any kind was recorded in south-east England for eighty-six years.* The only exception was a punitive raid launched by King Edgar (r.959–75) in 969 against the people of Thanet in the Thames estuary – a punishment meted out to the Anglo-Saxon populace for having roughed up some Scandinavian traders. The king, according to the thirteenth-century historian Roger of Wendover, was 'moved with exceeding rage against the spoilers, deprived them of all their goods, and put some of them to death'.[24] It is an illuminating anecdote, one which indicates not only the presence of Scandinavian merchants operating in the Thames estuary, but also the lengths to which an English king would go to protect them. Commercial contacts with the northern world were important and presumably lucrative, and as the largest market in the vicinity, London was undoubtedly the chief conduit for that trade and a major beneficiary of it.

For much of the tenth century, life in London continued as it had in Alfred's day. Within the walls, growth was modest beyond the western core, and the city north of Cheapside seems to have remained a wasteland. But the waterfront continued to develop, the gangplanks of the late ninth century replaced by increasingly solid timber

---

* Wars had been fought during this long interval, but they were fought ever further away, ever further north: in East Anglia, Mercia, Northumbria. Sometimes a ripple could be felt further south – the bishop of London, Theodred, a prominent public figure in his day, travelled north with Edward's son, King Athelstan, to fight against a confederacy of Dublin Vikings and other northern peoples at Brunanburh in 937. The battle was a famous victory for the king, and the bishop survived, but there is no way of knowing how many other Londoners marched north at the king's request, never to return home.

embankments built on the shoreline. Piles driven into the silt and tidal muck were reinforced with revetments – low riverside walls of reclaimed timber. Behind them the soggy slope was filled in with stones, mud and rubbish. Finally, planks were laid over the top: a flat and solid surface on which barrels rolled and leather-shod feet trod damply. A number of timbers found amongst the wooden remains of the embankments offer a glimpse of the commercial life of the waterfront, reclaimed material from the broken hulls of ships – the closest scrap to hand. This maritime salvage included the remnants of Anglo-Saxon vessels, parts from a massive Frisian trading ship (around sixty feet long) and fragments of boats that were built in the Viking tradition. It is impossible to know how these Scandinavian vessels arrived in London – perhaps they were brought by foreign traders, or built by immigrant shipwrights. Or perhaps they were captured, like those Viking ships that were brought to London in the 890s by the city's triumphant garrison – spoils of victory to be exploited until they passed out of use and were broken up for scrap.

The embankments are difficult to date closely, but the materials that were used to build them also offer a glimpse of the wealth that still flowed into the city. Most dramatically, they contained the remains of a building, constructed from trees felled in the third quarter of the tenth century: a massive timber hall of triple-tiered arcades, pillars and arches. It was a huge building for its time, over thirty-five feet high, roofed with wooden shingles, rising high above the single-storey dwellings that were still the norm. Informed by the decoration on surviving Anglo-Saxon masonry, it is appropriate to imagine that, like the

Scandinavian stave churches of later centuries it resembled, the timber surfaces of this building were smothered in elaborate decoration – brightly painted scrolls of vine and acanthus leaves, fields of elegant interlace, exuberant beasts trapped in foliate roundels, human figures frozen in their piety. It would have been dark inside, illuminated by tiny triangular windows that sent narrow shafts of light across the shadowed hall, catching drifting spectres of dust and woodsmoke in their pale beams.

No one knows for whom or for what purpose the hall was built. It possibly stood on land owned by the See of Canterbury or Worcester, and therefore may have had an ecclesiastical function – a church perhaps, or an episcopal palace. It reflects the fact that powerful interests were at play in the city: by the reign of King Edgar, assemblies of royal counsellors, senior officials and churchmen were meeting regularly in the city, and by the 930s London had the greatest complement of moneyers of any English mint – an economic niche that would underpin its growing status in the following century and foreshadowed its future fiscal pre-eminence. London in the tenth century was not the only urban centre in Britain, nor was it the most important. In the south, Winchester and Canterbury retained special status for Crown and Church respectively. London had foreign connections, but most of its trade – to judge by recovered pottery finds – remained domestic. It had some grand buildings, but most were small and some were squalid. It retained, however, a symbolic and commercial significance that sustained it in the face of disaster, a profile that kept powerful interests invested in its upkeep. In the year 962 a deadly fire swept through the settlement and burned down the venerable church of St Paul's.[25] Undeterred, the minster was refounded the same year, and the people got on with rebuilding their lives. London had become too big to fail.

But outside, beyond the dingy channels of the Thames estuary, a new storm was gathering; ripples of dark water building towards a surge that would break with all the mustered fury of the North Sea on the sleeping shores of England, to dash itself to pieces against the grim walls of Lundenburh.

III

Lundúnir

In 982 London burned again. It is possible that the city had, for the first time since 851, fallen victim to aggression: a Viking fleet raided Portland (Dorset) in the same year, and the *Chronicle* places the two events side by side. But even if the fires of 982 started innocently, the shadow of violence was once more looming over southern Britain. The raid on Portland was followed by an attack on Watchet (Somerset) in 987. But it was in 991, when a formidable Viking fleet arrived off the south coast, that the situation became suddenly critical. Led by a warlord named Olaf, this fleet achieved a great deal of harm in a short space of time. Arriving first in Kent, the Vikings ravaged Folkestone and Sandwich before moving on to Suffolk and laying waste to Ipswich. From there the fleet travelled south to Maldon in Essex, entering the Blackwater estuary. The Vikings were met by an East Anglian army led by the ageing Ealdorman Brihtnoth. The subsequent battle became a famous encounter, immortalized in Old English verse: a heroic, tragic elegy to doomed English resistance and a memorial to the silver-haired warrior who fell there, surrounded in death by his most loyal retainers.[1]

Glorious defeat may be a good subject for poets, but it is rarely good news for kings. For the English King Æthelred, the defeat at Maldon in 991 set in train a sequence of unfortunate events that would ultimately lead to his immortalization as Æthelred 'the Unready' and a reputation as an archetypically Bad King. The nickname actually derives from a late effort in Old English waggery: the literal meaning of *Æthelræd* is 'noble-counsel', but to the learned scribes of the 1180s this seemed so ill-fitting a name that the epithet *Unræd* – 'bad-counsel' – was appended to it. Thus to posterity he became known as *Æthelræd Unræd*, Æthelred 'the Ill-advised'. The account of Æthelred's reign that gave rise to this unflattering onomastic portrait was preserved in the C, D and E manuscripts of the *Anglo-Saxon Chronicle*, and was manifestly hostile. Nevertheless, it seems likely that much of the advice the king received was indeed deeply questionable, and that he was largely unprepared for what was coming over the horizon.

Æthelred, then, was both ill-advised and unready, with these two routes towards calamity converging in the king's habitual reliance on a character known as Eadric Streona – Eadric 'the Grasper' – a man of humble origin who rose to become ealdorman of Mercia in 1007 and, from 1009, Æthelred's son-in-law. In the eyes of Æthelred's hostile chronicler, evidence of Eadric's perfidy and cowardice was apparent early on. In 992, Æthelred's plan to thwart the raiding fleet by gathering to London all 'those ships that were worth anything' (presumably with the aim of trapping the Vikings in the Thames estuary) was scuppered by Eadric, who (allegedly) passed details of the plan to the Viking army before making himself scarce. The fighting, when it came, compounded the disaster: the Vikings – as was their habit – 'made a great slaughter'.[2]

It was probably only a matter of time before this water-borne horde turned its attention to London, the richest prize on the river. On 8 September 994, the feast of the Nativity of St Mary, the fleet came to London with ninety-four ships. The host was led by two men, named in the *Anglo-Saxon Chronicle* as Olaf and Svein, who came with the intention of burning the city. Olaf we have met before (he led the army that triumphed at Maldon in 991), and Svein we shall meet again. Both would ultimately rise to be kings in their native lands: Olaf as Olaf Tryggvason, king of Norway, Svein as Svein 'Forkbeard', king of Denmark. In 994, however, they badly underestimated their foes. At a time when English armies were routinely crumbling in the face of aggression and English towns burned like beacons wherever Viking armies marched or their ships moored, Svein and Olaf finally found a city of people determined and pugnacious – willing and able to bloody the noses of those who tried to harass them. In their assault on London Olaf and Svein 'suffered more harm and injury than they ever imagined that any town-dwellers would do to them'.[3]

This was not the end of this Viking host – in the months that followed it wreaked, in the words of the chronicler, 'indescribable harm' across south-east England – but it set a pattern for London's role in the years ahead. In 1009 another marauding Viking host, led by a formidable warrior known as Thorkell 'the Tall', settled on the Thames for the winter, sustaining themselves by raiding Essex and other neighbouring counties. Yet though the raiders 'often attacked London', the city would not yield so easily. 'Praise be to God it stands sound,' the chronicler exhaled. But perhaps no one need have worried: Vikings, as the scribe explained with the benefit of hindsight, 'always fared badly there'.[4] If the city couldn't be broken, however, it could still be squeezed.

Today, maritime Greenwich is a model village of riverside gentility, an elegantly poised memorial to enlightenment and empire: the home of the tall ships, dominated by a gleaming temple of white stone that served first to train the officers of the Royal Navy and, in latter days as the National Maritime Museum, to house their memory. The youths who passed through the Greenwich schools would go on to become the men who mapped and administered an empire – a world stitched together by mastery of wind and tide, of cartography and time. And above them, up on the hill, the astronomers of the Royal Observatory brought the heavens closer to the earth, clockwork motions traced with fine-grained precision, fixing time, charting the course of stars and planets – rationalizing and crystallizing the movements of the cosmos for the efficient operation of navigation and the reckoning of time, establishing the Prime Meridian of the world. Joseph Conrad imagined the

Thames as an outlet, a conduit from which 'the dreams of men, the seed of commonwealths, the germs of empires' spread outward into a darkly limned world. But the maritime history of Greenwich was set long before the enlightened barbarism of empire was unleashed from the maw of the river: 'Hunters for gold or pursuers of fame, they all had gone out on that stream, bearing the sword, and often the torch.'[5] A thousand years before Conrad wrote *Heart of Darkness*, that tide of fire and steel had flowed the other way. In with it came people with the will and nerve to plunder and exploit, bringing a dark flame from the outer world towards the heart of the Anglo-Saxon realm.

In 1012, a fleet of sailing ships moored at Greenwich: sleek wooden hulls and furled square sails of wool and linen, tall masts and brightly painted prows. This was the place a Viking army had chosen for its winter camp, a campaign stop after a season of raiding around the south coast – a series of devastating attacks that had resulted in the kidnap of the archbishop of Canterbury, Ælfheah. These Vikings, led by Thorkell, were using their presence at Greenwich to extort a massive protection payment from the English, and also hoped to ransom the archbishop back to his people. But as the months dragged on and the winter deepened, a frustrated malaise seems to have grown. Upriver, within London's walls, the hammers of the moneyers beat relentlessly down on coin dies, stamping out a river of silver pennies as the city – under the authority of Eadric Streona, at that time back in the good graces of King Æthelred – sweated to raise the vast sum of £48,000 to pay off the Vikings. And all through that winter the ships languished downriver at Greenwich, like reptilian monsters infesting a primordial lagoon, flopping in the shallows; and stretched out on the riverbank, a spreading rash of bored fighting men, waiting for silver and the spring through short grey days and damp river mists.

The battle of Maldon in 991 had been a pivotal moment in the history of the later Viking Age, and a crucial watershed for London's significance as the tenth century approached its close. In the aftermath of the battle it was decided – apparently on the advice of Sigeric, archbishop of Canterbury, but with the authority of the English king Æthelred – that the Viking army should be paid £10,000 in the hope that it would depart. It did not, and a second payment of £16,000 was paid after the events of 994. These tributes grew ever larger: £24,000 in 1002, £36,000 in 1007, and now, in 1012, £48,000. Even this, as we shall see, was not the end of it. For Viking armies at the beginning of the new millennium, the wealthy English state had become a piggy bank: it seemed that the more vigorously they beat it on the bottom, the more silver they could shake out of it. We do not know whether the payments were actually as large as the *Chronicle* describes – the figures are so vast as to have provoked incredulity in many historians. Nor do we know how the payments were made – in silver coins, in mixed treasures, or in kind. But even if only a proportion was paid in silver pennies, the scale of production would have had to be enormous. The numismatic evidence tells its own story – many times more English coins of this period have been found in Scandinavia than in the island where they were struck.

With 240 pennies to the pound, the tribute of 991 would

– if paid in minted coins – have required 2,400,000 individual silver pennies to have been produced; that of 1012 would have needed 11,520,000. Each one of these coins had to be hammered out by hand in the workshops of English moneyers. Nor were these the only demands that the English state had for coins: Æthelred's troubled reign demanded that armies be raised and equipped, and though many of those who fought were under obligation to provide their service and their war gear, mercenaries had to be paid and their provisions secured. There were also defences to be strengthened, bridges and roads to be maintained, ships to be built; many of these things involved labour that Æthelred could extract from his subjects, but costs were inevitable. Dozens of mints, from Chester to Canterbury, Winchester to York, Gloucester to Lincoln, would have laboured to produce the volumes of coinage that the king demanded – but none produced as much as London.

Between the 970s and the 990s the London mint, along with its sister mint at Southwark (see below), grew to dominate English coin production. The number of active moneyers increased dramatically, from the ten who were engaged in producing King Edgar's 'Reform' type (973–5) to the fifty-four who worked on King Æthelred's 'Crux' pennies (991–7). This explosion in personnel may represent something in the order of a five-fold increase in the volume of coins manufactured at London and Southwark – substantially more than the outputs of Lincoln, Winchester or York, the next three largest mints in the country. Although output subsequently slowed over the following two decades, London remained pre-eminent and would remain the most important centre of national coin production until the eve of the Norman Conquest.

London in 1012 was, therefore, the natural place to raise large sums of protection money; the English knew it, and so did the Vikings – it was not by accident that they had lighted on Greenwich for their bully-base, their intimidation-station. In the end, after what must have been a grim and stressful winter, Eadric managed to wring the necessary funds from the city, and the tribute was ferried downriver to the waiting Viking horde. It came, however, too late for Archbishop Ælfheah. It was said afterwards that, due to his tremendous holiness and enthusiasm for martyrdom, the archbishop had refused to allow any ransom to be paid for him. This did little to endear him to his captors. One rowdy evening, probably after a bout of indulgent feasting, the bored and listless Vikings decided to take out their frustration by hurling bones and cow heads at their captive. The *Anglo-Saxon Chronicle* reports the predictable outcome with an air of resignation: a Viking (named Thrum, according to a separate account) hit the archbishop over the head with the blunt end of an axe, sending – in the euphemistic phraseology of the chronicler – 'his holy soul to God's kingdom'.[6] In a half-hearted attempt at explanation, the chronicler offers that the killers 'were very drunk because there was wine' – brought, he tells us, 'from the south'. Perhaps this was booze intended for London markets, intercepted on the river by opportunistic bandits from the pirate port at Greenwich. It was meant to be quaffed by bishops and reeves, moneyers and merchants, not to lubricate the dry throats of episcopicidal Vikings.

After the archbishop's death – whether in the immediate

aftermath or much later is not known – a church was raised on the supposed spot of his martyrdom, at the heart of a Viking camp, beside a pagan hearth. The collapse of that medieval church resulted in its replacement in 1714 by the current building – one of a constellation of neo-classical churches that Nicholas Hawksmoor designed in the service of The Commission for Building Fifty New Churches, and mythologized in seminal psychogeographies by Iain Sinclair and Peter Ackroyd. In Ackroyd's *Hawksmoor*, the architect's fictional alter-ego Nicholas Dyer reveals to the reader his hidden intent to provide the Greenwich church with a human sacrifice, timed to coincide with the solar eclipse predicted by John Flamsteed, the astronomer royal (who looked down, but more frequently up, from his vantage point at the nearby observatory). Dyer need not have troubled himself: the sacrifice had already been made. The new church of St Alphege (Ælfheah) continues its vigil: an alabaster dreadnought of stone 'built', in Sinclair's words 'for early [eighteenth-]century optimism, erected over a fen of undisclosed horrors, white stones laid upon the mud & dust'.[7]

Ælfheah's body was reclaimed by the bishops of Dorchester and London (Eadnoth and Ælfhun) and brought back for burial to St Paul's, where, inevitably, it immediately began working miracles. The Viking army, with its plunder secured, broke up and its constituent parts went their separate ways. Thorkell took his contingent into the employ of the English king, promising Æthelred, with no small irony given Thorkell's devastating exploits of 1009–12, 'that they would guard this country'.[8] It was claimed by a contemporary German writer, Thietmar of

Merseberg, that Thorkell – having been converted to Christianity by the inspirational presence of Ælfheah – had been appalled by the drunken murder of the archbishop; that he had, in fact, offered all he had (apart from his ship) to try to prevent his death. How a monk in East Saxony should have come by this insight is unclear, and it may be that, having received his protection money, Thorkell saw greater opportunities for pay and reward in royal service than in continued piracy. Whatever the truth, it wasn't long before his loyalty would be put to the test.

Of the people who batted off Viking raids in 994 and 1009 there is not much that can be said. They were the descendants of men who had dragged captured Viking ships back to London wharves in triumph, of those who accompanied Bishop Theodred to prevail against the heathen on the famous lost battlefield of Brunanburh. They also, perhaps, retained their own memories of independence in the face of overreaching kings and presumptuous bishops all the way back to the time of Mellitus and the days of the old settlement of Lundenwic in the west. Violence was part of their inheritance, part of the civil fabric. Earlier in the tenth century the law in London had been enforced – at least in part – by the 'peace-gild'. This was a polite way of describing what was in effect an unofficial (though royally sanctioned) vigilante death squad – an association of private citizens whose self-appointed task was to hunt down malefactors (thieves mostly), extract property from them in recompense, and then kill them. Killing the guilty party (as well as 'those who fight with him and support him') was, in fact, particularly encouraged: those who spilt blood could claim an extra bounty of 12 pence.[9] Descriptions of the various provisions made for mounted pursuit beyond the city, and for dealing with larger groups of outlaws (including calling in reinforcements 'so that the guilty men may stand in greater awe'), make it clear that the activities of the peace-gild could closely resemble fully militarized sorties.[10] This was justice of the Wild West variety, with all the mayhem and disregard for human life such an image implies.

The peace-gild provides a glimpse of the sort of organization and experience that underlay the bellicosity of the Londoners in their dealings with threats to order and prosperity; but it is hard to imagine how manpower alone could have repelled serious armed incursions like the raids of 994 and 1009. The city also had to be fortified. Alas, archaeological evidence for reinforcement and maintenance of the defences is scant. Another church dedicated to bishop Ælfheah – St Alphege Cripplegate, also known as St Alphege London Wall – once concealed remnants of late Anglo-Saxon stonework beneath its north wall, before these were exposed by bombing during the Second World War. The church had been built hard up against the Roman wall, and may have overlain or formed part of late-Anglo-Saxon efforts to strengthen and improve this section of the defensive circuit. The church, however, must have been built some time after Ælfheah's death in 1012, and these remains may therefore have little to say about the walls that Viking armies assailed. More indicative evidence of the measures taken to fortify London has been found in traces of ditch-work outside the wall near Ludgate, Aldersgate and the Old Bailey.

The typical perimeter of the new-build Anglo-Saxon burh was comprised of a ditch and bank, the latter reinforced on its outward side with a stone or timber facing wall. Such arrangements, with ditches up to seven feet deep and banks up to ten feet high, are known from the ninth century onward at places like Wallingford, Oxford, Hereford and Cricklade. Where walls already existed (as at London and a number of other former Roman settlements), any new ditch-work would have fronted the extant defences. Apart from presenting a serious obstacle to attackers in their own right, ditches effectively raised the height of the walls behind them. It is reasonable to assume that London's surviving Roman walls were repaired and strengthened, perhaps heightened with new courses of stone or timber reinforcement (as at Bath), but if so nothing of this survives. Whatever defensive scheme one cares to envisage – and there are several different approaches that Anglo-Saxon engineers tried out across England – the effect would no doubt have been both impressive and intimidating.

The defences were also effective. In 1013, Svein 'Forkbeard' returned to England. This time he arrived as king of Denmark, with all the power and resources that his status commanded. It was a decisive step change in the nature of Viking incursion – no longer a private adventure undertaken by a confederation of freebooting warlords, this was an invasion, a war of conquest launched by a hostile nation. The speed of the English collapse was as swift as the scale of the danger was unprecedented. Wherever Danish banners flew the English submitted to Svein's authority. Everywhere except London.

The Danish army approached from Winchester: that city – the place most associated with the West Saxon royal house, the resting place of Alfred's bones – had fallen without a fight. Svein had every reason to feel confident, but his assault got off to a bad start: 'a great part of his people were drowned in the Thames, because they did not look out for any bridge', the chronicler mysteriously informs us (perhaps, though it is hardly clear, the army was forced to attempt a dangerous crossing from the south bank at an unpropitious point of departure). Demoralized and bedraggled, the Danish army found a city unwilling to capitulate. Unlike those of Oxford and Winchester, 'the inhabitants of the town would not submit, but held out against them with full battle because King Æthelred was inside, and Thorkell with him'.[11]

The chronicler, however, had otherwise precious little good to say about the beleaguered King Æthelred, and even this apparently approving remark might conceal a sneer. For centuries Anglo-Saxon rulers had been expected to lead their people into the open field: the triumph and tragedy of battle, fought face-to-face amongst the 'cracking of shields, attacking of warriors, cruel sword-chopping', had secured the legend of many a king. Anglo-Saxon poetry is replete with gung-ho vignettes: Cynewulf's *Elene*, a ninth-century verse retelling of the deeds of the Emperor Constantine – the prototype for Christian warrior kings – and his mother, articulates the ideal. When 'the approach of the Huns became evident to the citizens', Constantine 'ordered soldiers to be mustered with great haste in the face of the assault, to battle against the savage foes, and warriors to be brought to the attack under the open skies [. . .] Relentless of purpose onwards they trod; eagerly they advanced. They broke down the shield barrier, drove in their swords and thrust onwards, hardened to battle.'[12]

The image that the chronicler conjures, of Æthelred skulking behind the city walls with his Viking ally while the townsfolk bravely fend off the threat from without, conspicuously fails to live up to this heroic ideal of kingly warfare. The subtext – that the king was inept, kept shady company and was possibly a coward – is implicit in much else that the chronicler wrote about Æthelred's reign. Instead it is the Londoners who gain glory from this episode: once again they had shown themselves a force to be reckoned with. (Indeed, their reputation was becoming so potent that when Æthelred's son Edmund tried in 1016 to raise a fresh force to counter the Danes, the new army refused to fight without the London garrison beside them.[13]) The fortitude of the city's warriors, and the strength of its walls, had made London a rock against which Viking armies would continue to break, a rare outcrop of stoicism in a swamp of defeat.

Svein gave up the assault and turned back west, securing the surrender of Wallingford and Bath, and then of the entirety of the rest of England. It was only then that the people of London grudgingly yielded to reality, submitting to Svein and giving up hostages, afraid – probably with good reason – that if they did not 'he would do for them'.[14] But it was a short-lived subjugation. Svein dropped dead in February 1014, five weeks after completing his conquest and becoming king of England. The English bishops and ealdormen reinstated the recently deposed and humiliated Æthelred, summoning him back from exile in Normandy for two more troubled years on England's bitter throne.

By the first decade of the eleventh century, London was on its way to becoming the place that Pope Gregory and King Alfred had dreamed it could be. No longer an empty symbol of Romanitas – a cracked shell housing an honourable church but precious little imperial splendour – the city had become one of the wealthiest and most formidable of England's defended settlements. In 1013 it had been the place that King Æthelred chose for his last stand; in 1016 it would be the place chosen for his burial. He died on St George's Day and was laid to rest with Archbishop Ælfheah at the church of St Paul, the first and last king of England to be interred within the city walls. There his body lay undisturbed for 650 years, until in 1666, like the rest of the medieval cathedral and its relics, his tomb perished in the flames of the Great Fire.

The choice of London for a royal burial was deeply symbolic – it reflected how closely the city had come to be associated with power and the idea of the English realm as a whole. London could now be identified with the body of the king – the personification of the nation. It was not in itself a decisive move, but another accretion added to an already gilded aura: having a royal body to lay beside England's first bishop-martyr gave the city a political talisman to hang around an already muscular neck, stiffened by military prowess, fiscal power, geographical advantage. Nothing crystallized this relationship between city, Crown and kingdom so crisply as the manner of the new king's ascent to the throne. With his father dead and swiftly buried and a new existential threat brewing to the east, Edmund – later nicknamed 'Ironside' – looked to the city for recognition, and 'the councillors who were in London, and the garrison, chose Edmund for king'.[15] Like a Roman general elevated to the purple by the will of the legions, Edmund son of Æthelred was made king of England within the city walls, his rule affirmed by the fighting men of London.

There were also, however, practical reasons for the city to host these consecutive rituals of burial and accession. At the time of the old king's death a Danish fleet was making its way westward up the Thames, a terrifying flotilla led by a young and ambitious Danish prince named Cnut, the first-born son of the late Svein Forkbeard. When Svein died, suddenly and unexpectedly in February 1014, Cnut's younger brother Harald had taken possession of their father's vacated Danish throne and Cnut had found himself dispossessed – shut out from his father's English conquest by the recall of the exiled Æthelred. He initially remained in England following his father's death, gaining support in the north and the east – those regions most thickly settled by Scandinavian migrants, most recently swept into the English nation by West Saxon kings – but was driven out by the resurgent King Æthelred. However, after a return to Denmark to gather resources and the support of his brother, he had returned in 1015 with a fresh fleet and a will to power.

The war that followed was exhausting and devastating. Thorkell the Tall swiftly took Cnut's side, his oaths to

Æthelred of 1012 forgotten. Eadric Streona did likewise, defecting to the Cnutists with forty English ships. Much as his father had done, Cnut swiftly secured large areas of the north and east (those regions that had already once submitted to him), while leading devastating raids elsewhere. He must have known, however, that he faced a formidable opponent in the young prince Edmund. He must have known too that there could be no victory while London was held against him, providing shelter and military muscle to the house of Wessex. The city had become the key to the throne, the fulcrum on which English royal power rested; and so, in 1016, all the major pieces on the board began to converge: 'Prince Edmund turned to London, to his father; and then, after Easter, the king, Cnut, went towards London with all his ships.'[16]

The fleet arrived at Greenwich at Rogation Tide (5–9 May), in the aftermath of Æthelred's death and Edmund's accession. The anonymous author of the *Encomium Emmae Reginae* (a rather flattering portrait of Cnut's family exploits commissioned by his wife Emma) claimed that the Danish fleet was so decorated 'that the eyes of the beholders were dazzled, and to those looking from afar they seemed of flame rather than of wood'. He went on to describe how 'the flashing of weapons shone in one place, in another the blaze of hanging shields. Gold shone from the prows, silver also flashed', and to boast that 'so great, in fact, was the splendour of the fleet, that if its lord had wished to conquer any people, the ships alone would have terrified the enemy, before the warriors they carried had even entered into battle. For who could look upon the lions of the foe, terrible with brightness of gold, who upon the men of metal, menacing with golden face, who upon the dragons burning with gold, who upon the bulls on the ships threatening death, their horns shining with gold, without feeling any fear for the king of such a force?'[17] Who indeed?

One might be forgiven for reading this as fantastical hyperbole, but the sheer size, technical precision and awesome capabilities of late Viking Age warships have been dramatically confirmed over the years. Archaeological finds demonstrate that later Viking ships were optimized for their function, with clear differences between ships intended for long-distance travel and transportation and those built exclusively for war. The latter were the true Viking 'longships' – narrow and streamlined, they sacrificed everything to deadly function: their length maximizing the number of rowing benches for speed and manoeuvrability, the hull streamlined to a deadly point, a dagger on the water. Rowers doubled up as warriors – arms that pulled oars could wield sword and axe just as well, bodies honed to whipcord tension by repetitive labour, bulging pectorals, biceps of steel. The longship was a death-bringer, an 'iron-studded dragon'.*

By the time of Cnut the longship had reached its apogee. The greatest Viking ship ever discovered, named *Roskilde 6* after the Danish fjord in which it was found, was constructed during his reign, in c.1025. The ship is enormous – at 120 feet it is longer than the *Mary Rose* – a

---

* This is just one of a huge number of poetic metaphors for ships found in skaldic poetry: this from Þjóðólfr Arnórsson's mid-eleventh-century stanzas about King Harald 'Hard-ruler' Sigurdsson incorporated into Snorri Sturluson's *Heimskringla*.[18]

troop carrier for a hundred warriors, so long that its keel had to be stitched together from two mighty trees. The resources required to build a ship on this scale were only available to the wealthiest princes. It was ships constructed to this sort of epic specification that had helped Cnut to ultimately win and hold a North Sea empire – a realm that stretched from Ireland in the west to southern Sweden in the east, and from the south coast of England to Norway's northern fjords. Such ships were a dramatic assertion of power, an awesome reminder of control over the resources required to commission them. And although the archaeological evidence for the decoration of Viking ships is sparse, the Norman ships depicted on the Bayeux Tapestry offer a glimpse of how they might have appeared to contemporaries: banners fluttering, the strakes of their hulls painted in vivid alternating shades of black, red and yellow, shields of many colours and patterns hanging at the gunwales, the heads of beasts, terrible and strange, glowering from the prows.

In 2014, *Roskilde 6* made its way to London. Not in war – not even up the Thames – but flat-packed in shipping containers, its fragile bones painstakingly conserved and organized for reassembly in the steel skeleton that had been engineered to hold them: broken and crippled, painfully resurrected from a thousand-year sleep. Even this ghost ship, this thing built more of absence than substance, overwhelmed with its scale, shrinking the British Museum's vast and brutal exhibition space and making chaff of the treasures that languished in its shadow.

* * *

For all its modern charisma, its red-brick hipster appeal, Southwark has long been the city's bastard child: a place for the unwanted, the unseemly, the unsafe. It has an edge. Part of it is the concentrated reduction of London history, compressed into its modest footprint as though a tight unseen circumscription has forced the weight of the past to pile up on top of itself. Dickensian coaching inns, austere Victorian warehouses and medieval ruins squeeze together like rush-hour commuters, face to armpit. Defunct wharves and alleyways channel a savoury miasma from the heaving cornucopia of Borough Market's stalls – beer, cheese, fish, bread, meat, olives, artisanal confections from hip urban farmsters – towards revenant Elizabethan monuments: the facsimiles of Shakespeare's Globe and Francis Drake's *Golden Hind*; the funk of spices, stale beer and fried onions drifts through the underways, vaults of drunken office workers huddled in rowdy conclave beneath the cathedral, worshippers at Friday-night temples. The area is thick with high history and low culture: the Clink Prison and the London Dungeon, heads on spikes, whores and dockers, syphilis and cross-dressing, ale and pies. When new things arrive in Southwark they rarely have elbow room, forced to conform to the contours of whatever is there already. When London Bridge station was redeveloped, the new train lines were pushed through the upper storeys of pubs and offices, hovering above narrow roads and markets; mutilating but not obliterating, truncating height but adding weight. The Shard is the inescapable exception. Like some glacial eruption it plunges skyward, vertiginous, from beneath the earth – a great crystalline spike of modernity. It is as though the weight of Southwark has forced a jet of incongruity up through the cracks, as though the pressure was finally too much to bear.

Anglo-Saxon Southwark was a very different place at its inception. Though Southwark had been occupied in the Roman period, a built-up area around the southern end of the Roman bridge, its first post-Roman mention comes in the *Burghal Hidage*, where it appears as a place known to West Saxon scribes as *Suthringa geweorche* ('the stronghold of the Surrey-folk').[19] There it is described as a defensible enclosure with a perimeter of nearly one and a half miles – enough to encompass the entire island on which Southwark sits, hemmed in by stinking bogs and tidal floodlands. The only actual archaeology from the first half of the tenth century, however, is a ditch – presumably defensive in intent – enclosing a much smaller D-shaped area to the north of the island. A single timber can be dated to a tree felled just after 953. The impression is of a place that seemed like a good idea on paper – a fortified plot that could coordinate river defences with the city over the water – but which, in reality, never got much beyond the planning stages: surveyors came and went, workmen dug ditches, but no one really dwelt there. Southwark in the early tenth century probably had something of what Marc Augé called the 'non-place' about it: a transit area, a space of unmoored comings and goings; an administrative solution – extant on parchment before it was ever inscribed in the earth – all mothballed security measures and seasonal shift work; a 'zone'.

That began to change in the second half of the tenth century, but the impression of Southwark in its earliest years remains mundane and fairly squalid, a population hemmed in by river ooze and riddled with internal parasites. Scatters of late Anglo-Saxon pottery and rubbish dumps show an increasing human presence within the defended enclosure. (Beneath the ruins of the later medieval palace of the bishop of Winchester – still standing in Southwark where Pickfords Lane meets Clink Street – Anglo-Saxon refuse pits were found that once teemed with the larvae of intestinal worms, an endemic hazard of pre-industrial urban dwelling.) It was with two major developments, however, that the urbanization of Southwark really began, easing its transformation into a real place. One was the establishment of a mint. London and Southwark were the only two mints in England that operated in such close proximity; they worked in tandem to produce the river of silver that flowed from the Thames crossing at the turn of the millennium. Some moneyers had exclusive operations on one side of the river, others maintained workshops in both. That they were able to do so speaks to the other, far more critical, development that Southwark and the mother city were beginning to enjoy: London Bridge – long decayed, its bones given to the river – had been built anew.

The Anglo-Saxon bridge was over fifty yards to the east of where London Bridge is now. We know almost nothing about it – what it looked like, how it was made, how wide it was, how it was maintained. Only a few large timbers from the bridge have been recovered from the river and dated to between 982 and 1032. That it was a wooden structure is not in doubt, but the only description of the bridge comes in a history – Snorri Sturluson's *Heimskringla* – written two hundred years later than the events it describes; it may, therefore, be a better indication of how the bridge (or *a* bridge) looked in the early thirteenth century than the eleventh. Nevertheless, it was clearly a formidable barrier, and it can't have looked very different from how Snorri imagined it: 'so wide that wagons could be driven over [. . .] in both directions at once', and heavily fortified, with 'strongholds and wooden breast-works on the downstream side that came up waist-high. And under the arches were stakes, and they stood down in the river just under the surface.'[20] Warriors manned the battlements, helmets and spear points gleaming in the sun, brightly painted shields blazing, banners flying. Even for Cnut's dreadsome fleet this was an impassable barricade. To cut the city off completely Cnut needed to sever its connection to the south bank and to control the river west of the bridge – if he could achieve that, then his warriors would be able to encircle the city unmolested and, he hoped, bring this last bastion of resistance to heel.

With a winning combination of unwavering resolve and lateral thinking, Cnut had his men dig a canal that circumvented the southern end of the bridge, deep enough to bring his ships around to the other side.[21] This was not the Panama Canal. The Danish ships of the eleventh century were shallow-drafted and narrow, and vast warships like *Roskilde 6* were probably not the norm. Nor was the soggy alluvium of the south bank's marshlands an intransigent medium. But to cut an arcing path from, say, London City Pier to Blackfriars by way of Borough station (assuming the route tracked the path of least resistance, around Southwark island making use of the Borough Channel, a waterway more than three hundred yards to the south of the bridge) would have meant tracing a distance of nearly a mile and a quarter. Even to a modest depth this was no small undertaking, and to do it under constant assault from the formidable London garrison must have required considerable fortitude. Many Danish sailors must have died to dig Cnut's ditch.

The siege of London in 1016 was a famous affair, remembered long afterwards in Old Norse literature. A recollection of it was composed in verse in the aftermath of the fighting, quite possibly by a warrior skald (poet) who took part in the siege. The poem is known as *Liðsmannaflokkr*, 'the ship-warrior's song', and is preserved (in somewhat misleading contexts) in later Old Norse sagas.[22] In it, the skald eulogizes the fearsome attacks on London's walls by Cnut and Thorkell, the violent energies unleashed, the transcendent qualities of sacrifice and bloodletting that occurred there. He revels in terrorizing the natives ('once again we feed the raven with the blood of Englishmen'), praises the blood-lust of Thorkell's warriors ('they did not fear the sword-song'), chafes under Cnut's restraining hand (like 'an elk enraged').[23] Though Cnut and possibly Thorkell were Christians, the poem is saturated with the dark imagery of the pagan imagination: a death-rich shadow-world where grim gods watch with detached satisfaction as the piles of corpses grow higher, where the riverside runs slick with blood, where ravens grow fat on the flesh of the dead. Thus, 'each morning, the lady sees, on the bank of the Thames, that swords are reddened – the Hanged Man's* raven shall not go hungry'.[24]

---

* 'The Hanged Man' = the god Odin.

The lady referred to is the person to whom the poem is addressed, the intended object of its boasting and its triumphalism. It is jarring – from a modern perspective – to think of these verses as romantic overture, a blood-soaked tribute to a woman who watches with approval the unfolding carnage. The violence is a prelude, a clearing of the path towards a leisured future: 'now the hard-fought battles are done, we can sit, lady, in fair *Lundúnir*'.[25] Danish warriors would indeed take their leisured ease within the walls of London, but not quite yet. For the siege, though the poet omits to mention it, was a failure, the attackers fought once again to a standstill by the ferocious London garrison (led by the veteran East Anglian Ealdorman Ulfcetel – that 'bitter beardo [i.e. giant] of the stone-fortress') before a relieving army led by King Edmund arrived to drive them off.

There is a troubling tradition in Old Norse verse that is echoed in *Liðsmannaflokkr*, a habit of personifying the land as a woman to be pacified and penetrated, violated into submission by powerful men and their violence. When Cnut eventually did take London it was by treaty, not by force. But he would not forget the intransigence of the Londoners, their resistance to his hard embrace.

IV

Lundúnaborg

Cnut's war with Edmund Ironside rumbled on throughout 1016, a bitter conflict that pitted English lords against each other and tore the young English realm open along some of its most recently knitted ethnic and regional scars. When, finally, the exhausted factions came to an accommodation at Olney in Gloucestershire, it was agreed that Edmund would continue to rule as king south of the Thames, and that Cnut would hold Mercia and the north. The fate of East Anglia was left unclear, but its ealdorman – the mighty Ulfcetel, the giant of fortress-London – had been slain in the recent fighting. The Danish army turned back to London and a separate peace was brokered with the city. Cnut's fleet reappeared on the Thames, and his army prepared to settle down for the winter. Fate, however, intervened. On 30 November 1016, Edmund, who was apparently resident within the city, suddenly died. A later tradition – almost certainly untrue – maintained that he was shot up the arse with a crossbow whilst sat on the privy (an undignified end and, one imagines, an unpleasant modus operandi for the assassin).

Thus Cnut found that he was able to complete his conquest without further bloodshed, mere weeks after having been fought to an unsatisfactory impasse. He was proclaimed king of England, in London, in the dying days of 1016 in the presence of the English clergy and aristocracy. He had summoned the *witanegemot*, a national assembly of bigwigs, evidently seeking the legitimacy that only this theatre of universal affirmation could provide. His concern with the security of his rule was carried through into his first acts as king, extracting agreement from the English nobles that the late King Edmund had expected no familial succession and that he, Cnut, should be recognized as guardian of Edmund's children. Early in the following year he gave thought to the wider government of England: Thorkell was made earl of East Anglia, replacing the deceased Ulfcetel; Eadric Streona was formally recognized as earl of Mercia. Eadric did not have very long to enjoy the fruits of his perfidy. Cnut summoned him back to London in December 1017, and 'because he feared that someday he would be ensnared by Eadric's treachery'[1] had the earl killed on Christmas Day at the royal palace (*in palatio*). His body was thrown over the wall to lie unburied, food for carrion beasts.

Despite Cnut's close association with London in the early years of his reign – the royal hall he evidently maintained, the yuletide courts he held there – the new king was no friend to the city. In the aftermath of victory Cnut had levied the astonishing tax of £72,000 on England, extorted from his new subjects to pay his armies and reward his supporters. But London was singled out for special treatment, hit with a demand for a further £10,500. It was recognition, perhaps, of the city's economic power: it continued to be England's most prolific mint, with seventy-nine moneyers working in London and Southwark at the peak of production in the early part of Cnut's reign. But Cnut also had an instinct for punishment and subjugation, as well as a keenly felt obligation to the men who had propelled him to the throne. Making London pay satisfied both demands.

The king also found other ways to demean the city. In 1023 he hit upon a scheme to dislodge the miraculous corpse of Archbishop Ælfheah from St Paul's minster and have it taken to Canterbury to be reinterred under the auspices of Æthelnoth, archbishop of Canterbury. This would have been a serious blow to the city: the spiritual prestige and material revenue to be gained from the pilgrims who might be enticed to visit a miraculous shrine were significant; by removing the holy bones, Cnut was cutting the city's purse strings. The *Anglo-Saxon Chronicle* describes the disinterment and removal of Ælfheah's remains from an unremittingly positive angle, presenting the events as a sort of joyful and dignified parade that passed off with 'great pomp and rejoicing'.[2] There are, however, curious omissions in this account – the absence of the bishop of London, or any other named London dignitary, is particularly conspicuous.

A later account of the events – the *Translatio sancti Ælfegi Cantuariensis archiepiscopi et martiris* ('the translation of

St Ælfheah, archbishop of Canterbury and martyr') by the monastic writer Osbern of Canterbury (c.1050–90) – paints a wildly different picture of what went down on 8 June 1023.[3] According to Osbern, the removal of Ælfheah's remains was a heist, a raid on the sanctuary led by King Cnut himself and Archbishop Æthelnoth, undertaken while the king's *huscarles* – his personal bodyguard – pretended to assault the city gates.

There is a hint of Hollywood about it all: it brings to mind scenes of commotion, shouting, garbled instructions; confusion, adrenal fever, pounding feet on hard-packed earth; the garrison scrambling, men dragging weapons from walls, chests, under beds, searching for helmets, tripping over dogs, children, cooking pots; all attention towards the gates, to the west – or the north – no one knows for sure. All the while, four men are padding softly along the dim and rutted road; distant cries reaching their ears, the thud of stones and arrows against timber. Somewhere a bell is being rung. Silently they slip into the church, lighting torches as they go: tomb robbers, crypt breakers, resurrection men. Swiftly, purposefully, they jimmy the tomb with a candelabrum, wincing at the grinding metal on stone; then a sharp foul blast, of sweet rot and heady perfume, *unguentaria* of scented oils planted to mask decay. Prayers are muttered, crosses signed, and the body is lifted, quickly, carefully, wrapped in cloth; and then back towards the river where a ship is waiting – a 'royal longship with golden dragon prows', open-mouthed, dripping silent venom. The sound of pursuit is closing in, growing louder, voices thick with anger and alarm – but it is too late, the gang is already away, beyond the reach of spears and arrows. The king grasps the steering oar as the archbishop cradles the corpse of his predecessor in the bilge.

Cnut was, apparently, so concerned about reprisals by the Londoners that he had the bridge blocked and soldiers stationed along the southern riverbank. These were not the actions of a king who felt secure in his power: if the story is to be believed, Cnut was, when contemplating the reaction of his London subjects, in danger of soiling his breeches. Whatever one makes of Osbern's account, however, there were good reasons for the king to feel nervous around the city. He was unlikely to have forgotten that London was the place that had resisted him and his father the most bitterly. It must have seemed to Cnut a most likely crucible for rebellion, a rich and well-defended city with a wilful and unruly populace. These feelings were, no doubt, a major factor in his decision to spend significant amounts of time there at the beginning of his reign, and to station a permanent fleet outside the city thereafter. The king couldn't afford to lose control, and nothing could be a more effective restraint on unrest than the physical presence of the king and his warriors; and there is no doubt that Danish immigrants were making their presence felt, leaving their mortal fabric to the London clay.

For the gods and heroes of Norse myth who sought to enter the underworld, a river had first to be crossed. Its name was *Gjöll* – 'rowdy' – and it flowed not with water but with weapons. There was only one bridge across *Gjöll*, and it was guarded by a giantess. Her name was *Móðguðr* – 'furious battle'. Another story, told by the Danish historian Saxo Grammaticus in the twelfth century, describes the journey of the hero Hadding to the underworld in the company of a witch bearing hemlock blooms. After passing through sunlit lands 'they came on a swift and tumbling river of leaden waters, whirling down on its rapid current divers sorts of missiles, and likewise made passable by a bridge. When they had crossed this, they beheld two armies encountering one another with might and main. And when Hadding inquired of the woman about their estate: "These," she said, "are they who, having been slain by the sword, declare the manner of their death by a continual rehearsal, and enact the deeds of their past life in a living spectacle." Then a wall hard to approach and to climb blocked their further advance.'[4]

The river, the bridge, the battle, the wall, the ghosts of fallen warriors, doomed to an eternity of conflict; it is tempting to read in these images a reflection of the Viking Age and its carnage – of the men sent sprawling to their doom beneath London's walls, or plunging to mail-weighted oblivion in the murky waters of the Thames.

For in the eleventh century the River Thames truly ran with arms. In the 1920s a great haul of weapons was discovered around the northern footings of London Bridge: tapered spears, a grappling hook, and massive axes that could cleave a man in two or strike the head from a charging horse, wielded double-handed with terrifying force. They are on display now at the Museum of London, a grim fan of death tools fished from the mire, the detritus of violence. There are plenty of ways in which these weapons might have found their way to the silt: some we know of – the assaults of 994, 1009, 1013, 1016 – and probably just as many that were never recorded; some, perhaps, that we cannot even conceive of. But all of them left their mark on the imagination, contributing to the tapestry of myth and legend that was spun in northern halls in after days. London loomed large enough in the Old Norse imagination that it was believed by some to have been established by Vikings; the tale of Ragnar Loðbroð includes the story of how the legendary king founded the city: it was called, as it is in most Old Norse saga prose, Lundúnaborg.

This retrospective sense of London as a Viking town – a place knitted into the identity of the old north – was forged in the eleventh century, a product of the ethno-cultural transformations that the age of Cnut and his sons brought about.

Six inscribed stones stand in a rough circle around the low howe of Runestone Hill, southern Sweden, brought together from across Skåne and assembled in 1868 to commemorate the founding of Lund University two centuries earlier. One of them was brought to Lund from Valleberga parish; its runes are cut on two faces of the stone in curving arcs, one of which surmounts a simple cross. In translation they read:

> Sveinn and Þorgautr made this monument in memory of Manni and Svein. May God help well their souls. And they lie in London.[5]

Nobody can say who Manni and Svein were, what they did in England, how they met their end; nor can anyone know who Sveinn and Þorgautr were, how they grieved, whether they felt pride or dismay for their lost kin. But from the style of the carving and the context of similar stones it is likely that Manni and Svein had come to London with Thorkell or Cnut.* Perhaps they had pelted Ælfheah with the heads of cattle, or fought against Ulfcetel at Ringmere, against Edmund at Brentford and Penselwood and Sherston and Assandun. Perhaps they had perished outside London's walls in the fighting of 1016, or lived long enough to see Eadric tossed over them, to enter the city victorious and take their leisure 'now the hard-fought battles are done [. . .] in fair *Lundúnir*'.[6]

Certainly the city remained a base for a warrior caste, a fraternity of fighting men who had made London their home in the aftermath of Cnut's victory – men, perhaps, like Manni and Svein, who had sailed for England and never returned to Skåne. These were the *liðsmen*, the ship-warriors: a new elite in London society, maintained by *heregeld* ('horde tax') until 1051 when Edward the Confessor finally decided to abolish it.[7] From their ranks came the men who wrote the verses of *Liðsmannaflokkr*, who had sailed with Cnut and Thorkell and other warbands from Denmark, Norway and elsewhere. They were ascendant in the city – the beneficiaries of the taxes Cnut and sons extracted and the newfound respect that their Scandinavian heritage afforded them. See them swaggering down Cheapside or lounging at the harbour-side, striding with the arrogance of conquerors over London Bridge with their embroidered cloaks flapping in the river breeze,

---

* Other stones, of a similar style and date, refer to these leaders by name.

copper-inlaid sword hilts glinting, axes chased with battling beasts, silver brooches, golden rings, fat coin purses jingling.

They were well placed to take advantage of the continuing economic expansion of the city. The waterfront continued to develop, with mounting evidence for ships of diverse origin excavated from the revetments of the embankments at Bull Wharf and New Fresh Wharf, and there is increased evidence for exotic imports – continental pottery, high-end Frankish jewellery, Byzantine coins, eastern silks.

Medieval trade is a subject that can be difficult to convey in a way that catches the imagination. It is hard to capture the gross and violent colour and stench, the profane hubbub and briny tattooed bodies of dock workers and foreign sailors, the baffling variety of peoples and tongues and clothing, of gods whose names might be taken in vain; the silver, gold, wool, silk, spices, wine, flesh . . . Here a Frisian woman haggles over the price of walrus tusks with a dodgy-looking Danish Viking with eye make-up and filed front teeth; there an Iberian Jew is speaking Arabic to a glum-looking Rūs whose enormous silk trousers flap sadly in the damp breeze coming off the river. A posse of Normans, their hair full at the front but shaved from crown to nape – hardcore reverse mullets, haircuts that led the historian Simon Schama to call the Normans the 'scary half-skinheads of the early feudal world' – are being harassed about unpaid toll duties by the port-reeve, his luxuriant moustaches bristling with self-importance; they stare at him insolently – he'll be first against the wall when the Conquest comes. Further along the waterfront, naked dead-eyed slaves huddle together in chains on the freezing dock-front, prodded by leering gangs of drunken Londoners who have clubbed together to buy a body to abuse. And above it all, the scream of gulls and the slap of water on slick black wood, the crack of sail rope plucked by the wind, the stench of rotting fish and exotic spices, the bell of St Paul's tolling in the distance.

In truth, there is no direct evidence that any of these characters would have been present on London's waterfront – and certainly not all at the same time. The image is a composite, drawn from the types of people known to have frequented trading emporia from the Baltic to the Channel between the tenth and eleventh centuries. But the inter-connectedness of the maritime world meant that contact – of a great diversity of people and goods – must have been regular if not routine. The settlement itself was also growing rapidly, both the area under occupation and the density of habitation, with new roads laid down fronted by narrow plots spreading beyond the old western core, north of Cheapside and eastwards. The extensive excava-tions at Poultry, a plot then on the western edge of the Walbrook that flowed through the city, bisecting it north to south, revealed that by the early eleventh century a street of rectangular plots containing small houses – most of them no more than ten feet by sixteen – had been laid out, their narrow frontages to the road. Within them were found evidence for iron-working, butchery and domestic living. Amongst the detritus were also found scraps of animal bone worked with trial carvings – incised doodles that mixed Anglo-Saxon with Viking art motifs, reflections of an Anglo-Scandinavian identity that was beginning to develop, taking root in London streets alongside the Vikings themselves.*

The Valleberga stone – the memorial to Manni and Svein – is one of around thirty stones found in Scandinavia to mention England or a place in England directly, though it is the only one to refer specifically to London (ᚱᚢᚾᛏᚢᚾᛆᚢᛦ – 'Lundunum'). It is not, however, the only memorial to London's Scandinavian dead. One of the most remarkable of all Viking Age artefacts to survive from the eleventh century is a tombstone found in 1852 in the vicinity of St Paul's churchyard. It is decorated in the Scandinavian Ringerike style, bearing in low relief a representation of the characteristic 'Great Beast', with another creature impossibly tangled around his spiral-jointed foreleg. They face away from each other, as if struggling to break free from the self-animate tentacles that ensnare them. When it was new, the patterns on the stone were picked out in a visceral scheme of black, red and white; traces of the pigments still cling to the limestone surface.

An inscription runs along one edge of the St Paul's stone, carved in runes: 'Ginna and Toki had this stone set up . . .'[8] The message is partial, suspended where the stone has

---

* This was the bounty that was revealed thanks to the tragic obliteration of the glorious Mappin & Webb building at no. 1 Poultry. In a supreme irony, James Stirling's replacement has recently been granted listed status – as if the preservation of this blot could somehow atone for the act of vandalism that destroyed its forebear.

broken away, just a fragment of what was once a larger tomb. Thus we shall never know the name of the person to whom this monument was raised – another insoluble mystery of London's Viking dead. It leaves us instead with the signatures of the living: Ginna and Toki, two people – a woman (Ginnlaug) and a man – of Scandinavian name who chose to celebrate in stone a heritage that spanned the North Sea, seeded now in London's crowded soil. The stone is evidence of a new elite, a community of both the wealthy living and the honoured dead, of those with the skill and knowledge of Viking craft and those with the means and the will to commission it.

It is not the only fragment of Ringerike-style carved stonework to survive from the city's late Viking Age. A grave slab – probably from a city churchyard, possibly St Paul's, maybe even from the same grave as the runestone – is now in the British Museum. According to the Norman chronicler John of Worcester, a distinct Danish cemetery existed in the city by 1040, and had probably been there for some time.[9] Perhaps it was associated with the church of St Clement Danes – *Ecclesia Clementes Danorum* – a church of pre-Norman origins with Scandinavian associations that have never been adequately explained. Another fragment of Ringerike-style stonework was recovered from the church of All Hallows by the Tower – one of the only London churches still to retain standing Anglo-Saxon masonry. One group of churches, however – those dedicated to St Olaf – exerts the greatest pull on the spectres of London's Viking past, drawing them through wormholes between eras, tunnels through the strata of the city's past.*

* * *

---

* These are not the only dedications that suggest Scandinavian cultural ties: St Bride's Church, Fleet Street, possibly gained its dedication to the Irish St Brigid through Scandinavian connections to Dublin, and the name of the lost church of St Nicholas Acons (Nicholas Lane) is probably derived from the Scandinavian personal name Haakon. The church of St Magnus the Martyr, on Lower Thames Street, is dedicated to the twelfth-century earl of Orkney who died c.1116. Its dedication therefore post-dates the Viking Age, but it speaks to an enduring Scandinavian cultural presence in the city.

One lightning-scarred night in the mid-nineteenth century, a hackney carriage departed Hart Street, in the City of London, passing down the narrow passageway beneath 'crazy stacks of chimneys [that] seem to look down as they over-hang, dubiously calculating how far they will have to fall'. The cab driver, a 'bottled-nosed, red-faced man', was furtively looking back over his shoulder towards his fare, suspicious as to what ghoul-craft might compel a man to travel at midnight in a thunderstorm to ogle the weird portal of the church of St Olave Hart Street, its gate 'ornamented with skulls and cross-bones, larger than the life, wrought in stone' and with 'iron spikes a-top of the stone skulls, as though they were impaled'. For the middle-aged man in question, however, the experience had been tremendously satisfying; he had found 'the skulls most effective, having the air of a public execution, and seeming, as the lightning flashed, to wink and grin with the pain of the spikes'. This was how Charles Dickens described his nocturnal visit to the church he named 'Saint Ghastly Grim' in *The Uncommercial Traveller*.

I first encountered St Olave's as I wandered aimlessly during lunchtimes spent exploring the edges of the city when I worked at the Tower of London. I stumbled on the church unawares, wandering from Pepys Street into Seething Lane, struck immediately by the 'attraction of repulsion' that Dickens described.

It was only later that I learned that the body of London's great diarist, Samuel Pepys, had passed through this skull-crusted gateway in 1703 to be laid beside his wife Elisabeth. St Olave's had been Pepys' parish church, and its survival marked the effective eastward limits of the flames of the Great Fire – the demolition of homes at Mark Lane and west of the Tower of London created a brake that effectively halted the eastward progress of the burning. Thus St Olave Hart Street preserves a rare chunk of medieval London, a relic of the old city that the fire failed to claim. The building that survives is based on its fifteenth-century incarnation, with additions from later centuries (including the morbid portal of 1658). The earliest part of the church is the crypt, which dates to the thirteenth century, and nothing whatsoever remains of the Viking Age church that once stood here. There is little enough of any medieval fabric above ground level in London, and practically nothing dating to the early Middle Ages. The Great Fire razed most of the medieval city; the Luftwaffe took much of what was left. St Olave's received a direct hit from German bombing in 1941, and the church was heavily restored in the 1950s. Part of that restoration involved the incorporation in the restored walls of a carved stone fragment. Brought from Norway to London by King Haakon VII (who had worshipped at St Olave Hart Street while exiled in London during the Second World War) and the bishop of Trondheim, the fragment had been part of the tomb of St Olaf at Nidaros cathedral, the resting place of Norway's patron saint, King Olaf Haraldsson. It was the closure of a thousand-year circle.

The cult of King Olaf Haraldsson had grown swiftly after his death in 1030 at the battle of Stiklestad in Norway, killed in combat by forces loyal to Cnut. He had, in truth, been a dubious Christian role model: a power-hungry warmonger who brutalized the Norwegian populace with a programme of killing, burning and mutilation designed to tighten his grasp on a forcibly unified realm. Nevertheless, soon after his death tales of miracles began to be associated with his corpse, and the legend grew of Olaf the holy martyr – a warrior king who had died to preserve the faith, integrity and independence of the Norwegian realm. Much of the impetus for his cult seems to have come from his household bishop, Grímkell. Despite his Scandinavian name, Grímkell had originally left England in order to serve Olaf in Norway. He returned in the aftermath of Olaf's death (he was eventually made bishop of Selsey, in Sussex, in 1038–9), and with him the promotion of the new saint's cult gathered pace. The earliest reference in English sources to St Olaf, the *Anglo-Saxon Chronicle* entry for the year 1030, was written around 1050; in Yorkshire in 1055, Earl Siwerd of Northumbria was buried in a church dedicated to 'God and Olaf'. Dedications to the saint and references to him in the English liturgy are also known from Exeter and Dorset in sources that can be dated earlier than the Norman Conquest.

In some ways it is curious, this enthusiasm for Olaf Haraldsson. He had, after all, been killed in battle with the forces of Cnut, and was in many ways a counter-intuitive choice for an English saint in the eleventh century. For the Danes and the English who were loyal to Cnut's regime, Olaf was a rebel who had died fighting the interests of their king; for the rest of the English population, one might imagine that any Viking warlord – however enthusiastically promoted – would have been a hard sell. Yet the facts are unavoidable: the Norwegian aristocrat Earl Siwerd – who was buried in the church he had founded and dedicated to St Olaf – had owed his position as earl of Northumbria entirely to Cnut; Bishop Grímkell – the original cheerleader for the Olaf cult – was brought back to England at Cnut's invitation, and probably owed his elevation to the Selsey bishopric to Cnut's son and successor Harold ('Harefoot').

Nowhere was the cult so widely adopted as in London. Six churches in the city were dedicated to St Olaf, both north and south of the river: St Olave Broad Street, St Olave Silver Street, St Olave Old Jewry, St Olave Hart Street, St Nicholas Olave (Bread Street) and St Olave Southwark (Tooley Street). Although the precise dates of their founding are unknown, all of the Olaf churches can be shown to have received their dedications to the saint by the middle of the thirteenth century, and some are demonstrably much older. For example, although St Olave Old Jewry was not mentioned until the early twelfth century, ninth–eleventh-century foundations of an earlier building were discovered there in the 1980s. Though suggestive, this doesn't necessarily mean – even if the remains were part of an earlier church – that the building was dedicated to St Olaf from the time of its construction. With the church of St Olave Southwark, however, we are on firmer ground: a priest, 'Peter de Sancto Olavo', associated with the Southwark church, granted land to Bermondsey priory in 1096.[10]

St Olave Southwark became a place of memory, a place of pilgrimage. A story recorded by Snorri Sturluson in *Heimskringla* describes how a French pilgrim, so severely disabled that he was reduced to crawling on hands and knees, saw a dream vision of a radiant figure who instructed him to go to St Olaf's Church in London. He did as he was instructed (the formidable challenges of the journey are omitted), but on reaching London Bridge was thwarted by the ignorance of the locals, who couldn't remember to which saint any of their churches were dedicated. Suddenly, however, as is the way in such tales, the pilgrim was approached by a mysterious stranger. This character offered to accompany him south across the bridge, up to the threshold of the churchyard. Thus they came to the gates, and the pilgrim rolled himself through. Rising to his feet before the church of St Olaf, he found himself free of all pain and impediment; the saint had healed him.

Of the mysterious guide, of course, there was no longer any trace, and so it is now with the church itself. Nothing of the early medieval church of St Olave Southwark – nor of any of the later churches that were built and rebuilt on the spot – is to be found today. Its location, at the western end of Tooley Street, is instead occupied by St Olaf House; an Art Deco building of unflinching modernism, it was erected between 1928 and 1932 as the headquarters of The Hay's Wharf Company to a design by the architect Harry Stuart Goodhart-Rendel. The church may have gone, but the ghost of Olaf still haunts this place. At the left-hand corner of the building, where it fronts onto the road, the outline figure of 'St Olaf, King of Norway' looks down, picked out in mosaic lines to a design by the artist Frank Dobson, glittering yet insubstantial.*

Walk west from here along Tooley Street and you will find yourself in a grey penumbra beneath the dismal southern footings of London Bridge; it wasn't this way in the Middle Ages. The bridge began further to the east, close to where St Olaf House now stands – where St Olave's

---

* A separate panel, like a church wall memorial, sets out a short version of the biography of the saint and his church.

church once stood. It would have stood up as a beacon to medieval pilgrims, to those going south seeking benediction, drawn by the guiding hand of Olaf's ghost. But many as they crossed the bridge would have felt the undertow of other stories in the murky green water, dredged to life by creaking timbers and the damp river breeze. One event in particular would have loomed large in the imagination, one Viking assault on London so far omitted from this book – omitted because it probably didn't happen the way that Snorri Sturluson chose to tell it; or if it did, it happened at a different time and for different reasons.

In *Óláfs saga helga* – 'the saga of Olaf the saint' – Snorri tells the tale of how King Æthelred, recalled to England to reclaim his throne after the death of Svein Forkbeard in 1014, was not warmly met. London, he tells us, was held by Danish warriors, loyal to their dead lord Svein and the claims of his son Cnut. Faced with their resistance, Æthelred was forced to make an attempt on the city by force. He was accompanied by allies – both native and foreign, including the young Norwegian King Olaf – who brought their forces by ship up the river, the way Vikings had come to London so many times before. London Bridge, however, as it would prove for Cnut in 1016, was no trivial barrier. It is from this tale that Snorri's description of its defences comes – its ramparts and towers, its submerged stakes, its defenders raining down 'weapons and stones [. . .] so heavily that nothing could withstand them, neither helmets nor shields'. Thinking to capture the southern bridgehead, Æthelred's army then assaulted Southwark, where 'the Danes had done a lot of work, digging a great ditch and placing inside it a wall of timber and stones and turf and keeping inside it a great troop'. Despite ordering a 'strong attack', King Æthelred, Snorri tells us, 'achieved nothing'.[11]

Lucky for him that Olaf was there to provide the sort of advice that Æthelred otherwise famously failed to canvass. Like a northern Odysseus, Olaf presented his stratagem in council with Æthelred and the other warlords, and the fleet made ready for an assault on the bridge itself. Olaf 'had great hurdles made of withies and of wet branches and had wickerwork houses taken to pieces and had these put across his ships far enough to reach over both sides. Underneath he had poles put that were thick and high enough for it to be possible to fight from underneath and for it to withstand stones if they were dropped on top. And when the army was ready, then they rowed forward along the river to attack from below.' The defenders did their worst, damaging several ships and forcing many to withdraw. But Olaf would not be deterred: 'the force of Norwegians with him rowed right up under the arches and put chains round the posts that supported the arches, and they took hold of them and rowed all the ships downstream as hard as they could'. The pressure of the tugging chains, coupled with the weight of the men and their supplies of weapons and stones, brought the bridge crashing down, sending the defenders fleeing north and south to the city and to Southwark, and a good number of them to the embrace of the river. Southwark fell to Æthelred's army shortly afterwards. 'And when the citizens saw this, that the river, the Thames, was won, so that they could not prevent the passage of ships up inland, then they became fearful of the passage of ships and gave up the city and received King Aðalráðr [Æthelred].'[12]

Snorri seems to have been aware that this all sounded a

bit far-fetched. He attempted to back his story with skaldic verses composed in Cnut's day by Óttarr *svarti* (Óttarr 'the Black') which describe how Olaf, the 'battle-brave tester of the serpent of the storm of Yggr [. . .] destroyed the bridges of *Lundúnir'.*** However, the context of this episode in Óttarr's synopsis of Olaf's life is unclear, and no English source makes any mention of these events in reference to Æthelred's return to England in 1014. Moreover, another of the eleventh-century verses quoted by Snorri – this time by Sigvatr Þorðarson – seems to describe Olaf fighting *against* the English. Sigvatr places the attack on the bridge before another battle in which Olaf fought the English at Ringmere in East Anglia – a famous battle against the formidable Anglo-Scandinavian ealdorman Ulfcetel. This battle is dated by the *Anglo-Saxon Chronicle* to 1010, and the leader of the Viking army on that occasion was Thorkell the Tall: it is likely that Olaf's attack on London Bridge was actually related to Thorkell's abortive assault on the city in 1009. It is ironic that, for a thousand years, the church of St Olave's Southwark and the building that replaced it may well have kept vigil beside the scene of King Olaf's greatest mischief.

As is probably apparent, it is easy to get lost in the weeds trying to reconcile Old Norse poetry, Old Norse prose and contemporary Anglo-Saxon sources.

* * *

---

* *tester of the serpent of the storm of Yggr* is a convoluted poetic metaphor (or 'kenning') for a warrior: *Yggr* = 'Odin'; Odin is a god of war, and therefore the *storm of Yggr* = 'battle'; the serpent of battle [*serpent of the storm of Yggr*] = 'sword', and the tester of a sword [*tester of the serpent of the storm of Yggr*] = 'warrior'.[13]

Whatever really happened and when, or whoever's side Olaf was on, the growth of his cult points towards one of the ways in which the culture of the city was changing in the half-century after 1016; London by the eleventh century, like much of Britain, had drifted northward in attitude and outlook. Trade, migration and language were pulling the increasingly interconnected parts of the North Sea world together, with religious, cultural and artistic ideas spreading without hindrance. Scandinavian names were becoming more visible, particularly amongst the upper echelons of society. During the reigns of Cnut and his sons – Harold I 'Harefoot' (r.1035–40), Harthacnut (r.1040–2) – and into the reign of Edward the Confessor (r.1042–66), the moneyers of London included many men with Norse names: Siwerd (Sigurd), Thorcetel, Ulfcetel, Gauti, Frethi, Grim and Thor. These names do not, in themselves, indicate Scandinavian ancestry (just as English names do not necessarily indicate Anglo-Saxon ancestry). But at the least they suggest that Scandinavian identities were increasingly visible, acceptable, fashionable, desirable. Moneyers were part of a well-to-do class who commanded respect amongst their peers – people of means and influence who sat on local assemblies such as the Court of Hustings (first referred to in the late tenth century, and which may derive from the Old Norse húsþing – 'house assembly') and other guilds and fraternities. They were not, however, at the pinnacle of local power and prestige. In London those roles were taken by officials of overlapping (and frankly ill-defined) authority: shire reeves, port reeves and stallers. By the time of the Norman Conquest, several of these positions were or had been filled by men of Scandinavian heritage.

The Scandinavian warriors stationed in the city also remained a force to be reckoned with. In 1035, when Cnut died, the claims of his son Harold were upheld by the *liðsmen* in London. These were, presumably, the same men – sixteen boatloads of them – who had been supported by a tax of eight marks (roughly two-thirds of a pound) per rowlock (i.e. per oar; per person) throughout the reign of Cnut and his successor.[14] Harold was Cnut's son by his first wife Ælfgifu (also known, confusingly, as Emma – the same name as his second and overlapping wife). His best-known (and widely reviled) achievement was to arrange (or at least approve) the gruesome torture-murder of Æthelred's son Alfred and his companions in 1036. When he died in 1040, at the age of twenty-four, he was buried at an increasingly important monastic church to the west of London known as the West minster (*West mynstre*).[15] The development of Westminster Abbey may have been Edward the Confessor's great work, but it was Harold son of Cnut son of Svein who was the first king of England to be buried there. It already had substantial landholdings. In the tenth century, by a charter of King Edgar, Westminster had been endowed with a great swathe of land, encompassing much of what is now Soho and Covent Garden – all, in fact, of old Lundenwic, a great chunk of modern London south of Oxford Street, from Mayfair to Farringdon. The character of its landscape is revealed in the Old English boundary clauses that describe the land, a place of fens, tree stumps, hollows and cow-fords. In Æthelred's day, in c.1002, the bounds had been updated to include a dwelling place, a monastic croft, an ealdorman's boundary, a gallows – all signs, perhaps, of the creeping redevelopment of west London as the agricultural hinterland of the Westminster monks.

Harold was succeeded as king in 1040 by his half-brother Harthacnut, Cnut's son by his second wife, Æthelred's widow Emma. Harthacnut had been king of Denmark since Cnut's death in 1035, and had disputed Harold's succession to the English throne. On Harold's death he came to England from Denmark to claim the throne with support from his Norman mother. One of his first acts as king was to have his half-brother's remains dug up and hurled into a fen – perhaps the place referred to as *bulunga fenn* in Edgar's charter, an area of boggy wetland in the vicinity of what is now Buckingham Palace. One version of the story records the dramatis personae involved in this episode of fraternal malice, a motley crew comprising Ælfric, archbishop of York, Earl Godwine of Wessex, the king's household servants Stir and Eadric, and his 'butcher' (*carnifex*; with the meaning in this context of 'torturer/ executioner') – a man called Thrond. Harold's body was later supposedly reclaimed by a Thames fisherman, 'taken to the Danes, and was honourably buried at a cemetery they had in London'.[16]

Anyone who employs a full-time torturer is not likely to be thought of warmly, and Harthacnut was no exception. He was remembered chiefly for imposing 'a very severe tax that was endured with difficulty'. The *Anglo-Saxon Chronicle* offers the assessment that 'all who had yearned for him before were then disloyal to him. And he never accomplished anything kingly for as long as he ruled.'[17] Which, as it turned out, wasn't very long at all. A guest arriving late to a wedding in Lambeth on 8 June 1042 would have entered to witness a horrible scene unfolding: a young, finely dressed man lying on the ground, his face red and contorted, eyes bulging from his bloated head. His limbs thrash and twitch convulsively. One guest shrieks, others rush over to him; many more remain rooted to the spot, staring as a widening pool of dark liquid spreads across the timber floor, spilled from the silver-rimmed drinking horn that he still grips fast in his final reflexive spasm of ebbing life. Harthacnut, king of England, had 'died as he stood at his drink', most likely poisoned by his own nobles. He was only twenty-four years old, the same age his half-brother Harold had been on his death in 1040.

The festivities which Harthacnut's untimely demise had dampened had been arranged to celebrate the marriage of Tovi 'the Proud' to Gytha, the daughter of Osgod Clapa (Osgod 'the Coarse'*). Both Osgod and Tovi are Scandinavian names (Osgod is an Anglicization of the Norse name *Ásgautr*; Tovi is a variant of the Norse *Tófi*). Both were major landowners in England under Cnut, and it is generally assumed that they rose to power and prestige as a result of the conquest. They were also both 'stallers', an elevated rank one below the level of an earl. The two men also had close connections with London: Tovi in his own right as a London staller, Osgod through his son Æthelstan and his grandson Ansgar, both of whom also held the office of London staller. Harthacnut's death in 1042 marked the end of Danish dynastic rule in England, and Edward

---

* Writing in the 1090s, a monk of Bury-St-Edmunds – Herman the Archdeacon – described Osgod wearing arm-rings on both arms and an axe slung on his shoulder in the 'Danish fashion'.[18]

son of Æthelred (later known as 'the Confessor') became king. But the families of people like Tovi and Osgod ensured that Scandinavian influence and cultural ties were maintained in the city in the decades after Harthacnut's demise.

The most significant of these families was that of Godwine, earl of Wessex. Despite his own West Saxon origins, Godwine was by far the most important figure in what was an increasingly recognizable Anglo-Danish faction in English politics. He had owed his earldom entirely to Cnut, most likely in recognition of his support in the wars of 1016, and was a firm backer of Harthacnut in the disputed succession that followed Cnut's death. He was, moreover, married to the Danish noblewoman Gytha, sister to Jarl Ulf Thorgillson, one of the most powerful men in Denmark. It was her influence that saw a church to St Olaf built at Exeter, and quite possibly the church of St Olaf at Southwark as well: Domesday Book records that Earl Godwine was the lord of Southwark in 1066, holding the land as a personal possession. The Danish sympathies of the Godwine clan were made plain in the naming of their children – several of them were given Scandinavian names: Tostig, Svein, Gyrth, Gunhilda and Harold, the future ill-fated and brief-tenured king of England.

King Edward the Confessor was at odds with Earl Godwine for the first ten years of his reign. Edward's animus is understandable – the earl had been largely responsible for the kidnap, blinding and subsequent death of Edward's brother Alfred in 1036. Godwine, for his part, resented the reduced Danish influence at court at the expense of Franco-Norman interests (it is telling that, around this time, references to 'foreigners' in the *Anglo-Saxon Chronicle* seem generally to imply French-speakers rather than to Scandinavians). King Edward outlawed Earl Godwine and his family in 1051, driving them to a campaign of piracy and coastal raiding that continued in the grand tradition of Viking terror. In the same year, the king significantly brought an end to the *heregeld* that had been levied since the days of Æthelred to provide for the *liðsmen* and other mercenaries. The people the *geld* had sustained, however, and their cultural affiliations, did not melt away overnight.

When the conflict between Edward and Godwine came to a head in 1052, it was Earl Godwine's Anglo-Danish faction that ultimately received the support of the Londoners. (The townsfolk were perhaps encouraged in their adherence to the Godwine cause by the close proximity of the earl's power base in Southwark.) King Edward's army approached London from the north, Earl Godwine's fleet sailed upriver like so many Viking fleets before it. Peace eventually broke out, but only because the city's inhabitants had come to recognize that their interests were better aligned with the earl's than with the king's; that 'they wanted', as the *Anglo-Saxon Chronicle* put it, 'almost all that he wanted'.[19] Faced with a hostile city, Edward had little choice but to come to terms with the wayward earl and pardon his past transgressions; the uneasy settlement lasted for the rest of King Edward's life. London, it seems, had been a base for Scandinavian warriors and their interests for so long that their loyalties could no longer be taken for granted by the English king, their traditions fusing with the age-old belligerence of the Londoners as the political intrigue around the English throne swirled towards the succession crisis of 1066 and the Norman Conquest that followed.

Earl Godwine died in 1053 and was replaced in power and influence by his eldest son, Harold. When King Edward died early in 1066, Harold was proclaimed king by the English nobility, setting in motion the events that led to the Norman Conquest of England. He died on the battlefield at Hastings, alongside his brothers Gyrth and Leofwine (Tostig had been killed a few weeks earlier at the battle of Stamford Bridge, fighting against his brothers as an ally of King Harald 'Hard-ruler' Sigurdsson of Norway). In the darkening days that followed the Norman Duke William's victory, the London garrison threw their weight behind the claims of Edmund Ironside's grandson, Edgar. But the city was essentially alone, abandoned by potential allies to the north (the earls Edwin and Morcar) and cut off from Godwine family lands in Wessex.

Nevertheless, London remained a daunting prospect for any would-be conqueror, its already independently minded citizens reinforced by the bitter survivors of Hastings. According to the *Carmen de Hastingae Proelio* (the Norman writer Guy of Amiens' versified telling of the Norman Conquest) London was 'a most spacious city, full of evil inhabitants, and richer than anywhere else in the kingdom. Protected on the left by walls and on the right by the river, it fears neither armies nor capture by guile'.[20] Duke William's knights assaulted the city and its environs on at least one occasion, devastating Southwark. They failed, however, to take the bridge, and the Norman army was forced to move on and cross the Thames at Wallingford.

Guy seems to have believed that William later made his

base at Westminster, which under Edward's rule had seen a dramatic investment of resources as a royal palace and religious house. There he 'built siege-engines and made moles and the iron horns of battering rams for the destruction of the city; then he thundered forth menaces and threatened war and vengeance, swearing that, given time, he would destroy the walls, raze the bastions to the ground, and bring down the proud tower in rubble'. The *Carmen*, alas, is not very reliable at this point in its narrative. But the description of William's rage remains an indication of how formidable, how impregnable, the fortress-city loomed in the contemporary imagination.[21]

Meanwhile, Guy relates, London's defences were being organized by Ansgar the staller, grandson of Osgod Clapa. Though gravely wounded on the battlefield at Hastings, Ansgar set about his task from a litter carried by his retainers, rallying the city militia to one last stand against the tides of time and the impending doom of Anglo-Saxon England. It was a final gasp of defiance, inspired by the unyielding scion of an Anglo-Scandinavian house. Any ethnic distinctions that persisted in the city had long been blurred by synthesis and proximity; now they were erased by crisis, smudged out in the red sunset of the Viking Age.

In the end, London's surrender was negotiated, political reality once again overtaking the city's taste for intransigence. The English nobility, the 'best men in London' amongst them, capitulated in December, at Berkhamsted in Hertfordshire. Subdual of London had become the essential prerequisite for effective rule in England, and shortly after the meeting at Berkhamsted steps were taken to formalize the completion of William's seizure of the English throne. Like Cnut, William was terrified of London. His fear is palpable in the thundered menaces and the threats of vengeance he supposedly spat from Westminster. But it was more viscerally on display in the final coda to the conquest of London, a flurry of violence born of Norman paranoia. At William's coronation, at Westminster on Christmas Day, Norman knights posted outside mistook shouts of acclamation for a riot. Nervous, inured to violence and primed to do what they did best, the Normans began setting fire indiscriminately to the buildings in the vicinity. As the fire spread and smoke billowed, those inside the church panicked, rushing out to fight the flames or to loot in the chaos as inclination and opportunity dictated. Only William and the officiating clergy remained inside to complete the consecration rite, the new king pale before the altar, 'trembling from head to foot'.[22]

Looking back down the river on Christmas Day in 1066, an Anglo-Danish refugee, fleeing like so many did from the trauma of the conquest, might have seen in the distance, beyond the wreckage of sacked Southwark and the flat marshes that bounded the southern bank where the river coils south, a red stain of burning on the ash clouds that rolled from Westminster; might have seen, as Marlowe did, that 'west on the upper reaches the place of the monstrous town was still marked ominously on the sky, a brooding gloom in sunshine, a lurid glare under the stars'.[23] London's Viking Age had ended in the manner in which it had begun, with smoke drifting on the water and fire lighting up the sky.

V

Vikings Drink Tea

Mr. Pickwick's eyes sparkled with delight, as he sat and gloated over the treasure he had discovered. He had attained one of the greatest objects of his ambition. In a county known to abound in the remains of the early ages; in a village in which there still existed some memorials of the olden time, he – he, the chairman of the Pickwick Club – had discovered a strange and curious inscription of unquestionable antiquity, which had wholly escaped the observation of the many learned men who had preceded him.

Charles Dickens, *The Pickwick Papers*

Many thousands of Viking Age coins are to be found in Bloomsbury, tucked snugly in their drawers at the British Museum, part of the nation's rich numismatic collection. Amongst them can be found the products of workshops striking coins in the names of Britain's Viking rulers – iconic coins made for Olaf Guthfrithsson (whose coins were the first in England, and perhaps anywhere, to use a version of the Germanic word for king – *konung* – instead of the Latin *rex*) or Eric Bloodaxe, struck in York by men with names like Brandr ('Fire') and Thor. There are coins produced by the Scandinavian settlers of eastern England: the pennies of Guthrum in the name of his Christian alter ego, Æthelstan; the crude copies of Alfred's coins, including the famous London monogram. Then there are those of Cnut the Great, the mightiest of all Scandinavian warlords, who issued coins as king of England in volumes rivalled only by his predecessor, the harassed and unhappy Æthelred. And of all the places that toiled to produce Cnut's currency, London stood pre-eminent.

Paper-thin discs of silver, the coins sit in small individual circular depressions – thirty or so arranged in rows on the wooden trays, like antique sets of Connect 4. Removing the coin – lifting gently with the edge of a thumbnail until the coin stands vertically on its edge, taking it between thumb and forefinger, placing it carefully to one side – reveals the ticket below. Spidery handwriting of a long-dead curator decorates the yellowing fly-blown circles of card, detailing the provenance, the dates of acquisition: 1838, 1889, 1915 . . . tiny handwritten documents that describe coins struck a thousand and more years ago. They are not the only record: from the mid-nineteenth century onwards, leather-bound ledgers record acquisitions to the collection – each line of meticulous calligraphy accompanied by hand-drawn illuminations of objects and inscriptions; a bittersweet memorial to a more leisured age of curatorial endeavour. They sit amongst the genteel decrepitude of mahogany cabinets and shelving, rubbed smooth by the passage of two centuries – a constant reminder of the hands and minds whose labour brought the Vikings out from the shadows of an imagined 'Dark Age'.

The end of the nineteenth century was a period distinguished by an apparently boundless enthusiasm for clubs, societies and myriad other forms of organized fraternization. It was also a high-water mark of the Viking Revival, a sudden and intense burst of creativity and scholarship inspired by the rediscovery of the poetry and history of the early medieval north. It should be no surprise that these two Victorian obsessions eventually converged, and The Viking Club, later The Viking Society for Northern Research, was founded in London in 1892. The Club had originally formed in 1819 as The Orkney and Shetland Society of London, an organization constituted for 'the relief of natives of Orkney and Shetland [and] their wives resident in London, in circumstances of difficulty or distress'.[1] These were doubtless worthy aims in the early nineteenth century, when the rural exodus to the capital generated an unprecedented demand for friendly networks. But by the end of the century the justification for such a narrow remit was fading, and it was determined that a change in emphasis towards the social and literary interests of young men of northern origin – 'music, entertainment, and plenty of opportunity for talk' – would be of greater general benefit. Indeed, in order to make the Society even more congenial to these wandering islanders, it was also decided – not without some controversy – that the 'book of laws [of the Society] should be made as characteristic of Orkney and Shetland as possible by the introduction of *the old names*',[2] a fateful injunction that was to have unintended, if not perhaps unforeseeable, consequences. Thereafter, members of the club were duly referred to as 'Udallers',* and meetings of the Society as 'Things'. The club journal would be (and indeed still is) known as the 'Saga-book'.

In a little over a year it had been decided that there were fewer roving and lonely northern roustabouts than had been anticipated, and membership was accordingly opened to anyone with an interest in 'Northern studies'.[3] Nevertheless, despite the loosening of the Society's entry requirements, the fervour for esoteric nomenclature only grew. A sense of how deeply these eccentricities ran can be gained by the thoroughness with which even the most abstruse bureaucratic arrangements were attached to anti-quated terms and concepts. Thus the Society not only substituted 'Great Al-Thing' for annual general meeting and 'Jarl' for president, but also insisted on referring to honorary district secretaries as 'Herath Umboths-Men' and trustees of the club property as 'Eign-Wards'. The honorary financial secretary was unfortunate enough to be burdened with the epithet 'Skatt-Master' – marginally less humili-ating, perhaps, than that of his underling the 'Skatt-Taker' (the 'honorary treasurer'). Members themselves swapped the obscure 'Udaller' for, simply, 'Viking'.

All of this enthusiastic tomfoolery made the Society an obvious target for mockery. The first meeting of the 'new' Viking Club took place on 12 January 1894 in the King's Weigh Rooms on what was then Thomas Street (now Binney Street) near Grosvenor Square, Mayfair.

---

* A 'udaller' is someone who has rights under udal law, a legal system of Orkney and Shetland with Norse origins.

Unfortunately for the Club, the event was crashed by a reporter for the *Pall Mall Gazette* who penned an acidly amusing, if slightly mean-spirited, article for his newspaper on 15 January entitled 'VIKINGS DRINK TEA'.[4] Apart from the narrowness of the road ('a nice width for swinging a cat in') and the interior décor ('large and reasonably lofty, with fawn-coloured walls [. . .] three skylights in the roof and thirty-five gaslights in the room'), the journalist's principal concern was how poorly the event matched his preconceived ideas of how a 'Viking Club' should comport itself. 'The reception was held,' he reports, 'by the Jarl, who is also the president of the club, and is known in private life as Mr. W. Watson Cheyne. Members and guests were introduced to him by the Law Man, who is also President of the Council or Law-Thing, and who is, in addition, the Things-Both-Man, or Convener. In spite of all these titles, nobody would pick him out of a crowd for a Viking, unless he wore a placard on his chest proclaiming the fact.' Equally disappointing to the reporter was the choice of refreshment, and the unseemly enthusiasm with which those in attendance assailed the cake and hot beverages: 'Had they borne any resemblance to the Vikings who sailed the seas, eight or ten centuries ago, there would have seemed something incongruous in tea for a beverage; but there was no resemblance whatever, and it seemed as if there could not be a fitter drink for most of them than tea.'

Journalists, it must be said, have never ceased to be dismayed by the failure of scholars to play up to their Viking fantasies. The merest briny whiff of longships is enough to prompt a rummage through the cliché cupboard in search of orange beards and horned helmets, blood, fire and battle-axes; the realities – of academia and of the Viking Age itself – can sometimes be a source of peculiar disappointment and even indignation. There is little doubt, however, that the adoption of 'the old names' had set up a larger than usual gulf between expectation and reality. On being told that the official Club pronunciation of the word Viking would be 'Weaking', the writer expressed a view that 'such a pronunciation was, of course, enough to make any admirer of the ancient sea-rovers lose all interest in the Viking Club' – a heartfelt dismay with which anyone might find sympathy.[5]

The subjects debated by the Viking Club in its earliest days veer from the learned and pioneering to the bizarre, the parochial and the laughable. Thus, alongside major scholarly contributions from the likes of the English antiquarian W.G. Collingwood (on the Cumbrian Viking Age), the Norwegian philologist Sophus Bugge (on the relationship between the Old Norse and Anglo-Saxon versions of the Wayland myth) and the Icelandic saga translator (and long-term collaborator with William Morris) Eirikr Magnusson (on the origin of the word 'Edda') can be found a number of more Pickwickian offerings. For example, a rambling disquisition from the Icelandic poet Einar Benediktsson concludes with a puzzling demand to know 'whether any old serpent-mounds had been found in Iceland, such as those on the west coast of Scotland and in the Hebrides. They were heaped up in the form of a snake, with flat stones to represent the head, and were no doubt a relic of sun worship.'[6] On another occasion, 'Mr. Geo. H. Fellowes Prynne, F.R.I.B.A.' was moved to biblical cadences by a paper given by the historian Frederick York

Powell,* and implored the gathered members to 'let not these precious remains be wiped out from the history of your noble country! No! It is by such links as literature and art that Northerner and Southerner are bound in one common interest and brotherhood. So let it be.'[7]

This sort of enthusiasm was not unusual. Alfred Heneage Cocks, for example, said that he 'took interest in every thing that concerned the Club, that is, in every thing Scandinavian'.[8] He then launched into a long description of his encounters with whales: 'In answer to a question as to whether he had tasted whale meat, Mr. Cocks said that he had eaten plenty of it,' and went on to enlighten the assembled party with the news that, having dined on the flesh and blubber of a three-months deceased Rorqual, this was 'certainly not *choice*'. (No doubt this *bon mot* left the thirty-five gas lights of the King's Weigh Rooms reverberating with antiquarian mirth.)

On occasion, however, the proceedings lurch without warning towards the grotesque. In another intervention on behalf of the Society, the aforementioned Mr Cocks described the indigenous people he met in Finland as 'dirty little savages'.[9] Cocks's evident affection for his subject, however, at least manages to elevate his discourse above the depths plumbed by the repulsive and improbably named Poulteney Bigelow, an American whose chief input to the Society was to observe of a Sami settlement in northern Norway that the 'chief thing that struck him [. . .] was the very distinctive Lapp odour that pervaded it, which, after

---

* 'Some Literary and Historical Aspects of Old Northern Literature'; no record of the content of Powell's talk survives.

he had been holding a Lapp baby, he did not get rid of for some time'. As if this were not sufficiently absurd and offensive, he went on to pronounce that 'all over the world each race has a characteristic race odour. This was the case, for instance, in America, where [. . .] the whites dislike the "negro smell".'[10] (Mr Bigelow, it is worth noting, was an early fan of Hitler and a lifelong friend of Kaiser Wilhelm.)

For the most part, however, meetings of the Society in the 1890s were light-hearted and genial affairs, able on occasion to boast attendance from towering figures of late-Victorian cultural life. A late arriver at the Society's meeting of 11 January 1895, still wrapped in an envelope of cold and the brief perfume of the winter street, would have found a familiar figure in the chairman's seat. After an embarrassed fluster of shed outer clothes, perspiration breaking out amidst the sudden warmth of radiating anti-quarian bodies, nose red and hands numb, he or she might have noticed that the chairman (or 'Thing-Seat-Man' to give him his proper title), though only sixty, looked older – his unruly beard winter-white, his hair erupting haphazardly like candyfloss in every direction from his head. The skin of his face is baggy, too big for the skull behind it, and lines crease his forehead; but the eyes still twinkle with undiminished starlight. 'No history,' he is saying to the group gathered around him, 'is more complete than popular mythology, because at the time when people were under the influence of superstition they had not learnt the art of lying, or, if they did lie, they did it so transparently that it was very easy to read between the lines and divide the true from the false.' He smiles a sly little smile, the creases deepening around his eyes: 'So one might say that folklore represents absolutely truthful lies, and therefore stands in complete opposition to the ordinary newspaper article.'[11]

William Morris would die in October of the following year, aged sixty-two. His obituary in the Saga-book records that he was elected as a 'Jarla-man' (vice-president) in 1893 and as 'Skald' (poet) and 'Fræthi-man' (honorary fellow) in 1895, and goes on to list the work that ensured his place in Old Norse historiography: '"The Lovers of Gudrun", founded on the Laxdaela Saga, "Sigurd the Volsung", which appeared in 1876; a prose rendering of it [. . .] under the title of "The Story of the Volsungs and the Niblungs"; and "Grettir the Strong" in 1869, and "Three Northern Love Stories" in 1875 [. . .] versions of the Eyrbyggja Saga, Heimskringla, etc., etc. [. . .] He took an active part in the work of the Viking Club, and last acted as the Chairman for the evening on Jan. 11th, 1895.'[12] There are few individuals who have contributed so much to the popularization of the Viking past.

The visitor to Thomas Street, or Binney Street as it is now, will find it much as the reporter for the Pall Mall Gazette described it: narrow – narrower now, indeed, with designated parking running up its western flank. It feels more claustrophobic than it should thanks to the hard, high red bulk of the King's Weigh Rooms and Chapel pressing down from the west, its quasi-Romanesque architecture a bluff advertisement for the Victorian preoccupation with God, empire and good breeding. It is an odd style, the earnest heft of red brick and yellow stone an exercise in medievalism that succeeds only in evoking nostalgia for its own revivalist age. Walking the streets

thereabouts one finds the nineteenth-century fabric of
Mayfair rolling out in genteel banality in every direction
– Weighhouse Street, Duke Street, Brown Hart Gardens,
Grosvenor Square – until, turning to the west, one is at
last confronted by the awesome, terrifying bulk of the
former US Embassy building.* It is another cocksure
display: a monument to the age of McCarthy and
Eisenhower, its arrogant lines thrusting American vitality
in the face of the old world.

There is little here to speak to the Viking enthusiast –
no hint of grim northern gods or swan-necked dragon-ships.
And for the members of the Viking Society, their immediate
environs were of little consequence. All of their energy was
turned northward, towards Orkney, Shetland and beyond
– towards a dimly perceived Thule, a land of ice and snow
and dragons. Theirs was a Viking world of myth and legend,
always a faraway land. In 2017 I went with my wife to
Water House, where Morris had lived as a teenager, in
Walthamstow near the River Lea; it is now the William
Morris Museum. I had gone to hear extracts read from
Lavinia Greenlaw's edition of Morris's journal describing
his first visit to Iceland in 1871.[13] Morris's journey was a
pilgrimage of sorts, an opportunity to find the images that
fitted his 'old imaginations of places for sea wanderers to
come to' and to grasp 'the thin thread of insight and imagination' that sight of the rifts and peaks of Iceland brought
within his reach. As we absorbed extracts of Morris's prose,
interspersed with fragile and ethereal songs performed by

---

* Designed by Finnish-American architect Eero Saarinen, and completed
in 1960.

the Icelandic singer Ösp Eldjarn, I reflected on the irony of Morris's northern longing – the fact that he had travelled so far from home to find what his imagination craved. Yet close to the house where we sat, the child Morris, astride a pony and encased in a miniature suit of armour, had mounted expeditions deep into Epping Forest, patrolling the wild borders of the Danelaw, east of the River Lea where Viking ships once sailed.

For Morris and his peers, London and its suburbs were merely points of departure and of bitter-sweet home-coming: the city contained little that could hold the attention of men and women steeped in the hyperborean glamour of the sagas. But the past, like water, flows where it will, seeking channels that bring it ever closer, rushing up to meet us when we least expect it, rising from beneath the ground or inundating shores thought dry for miles and desolate. And even far-off places are brought surging close by the ebb and flow, springing out of channels long thought barren, and rushing past familiar scenes with sudden, deadly urgency. Though the members of the Viking Society seem not to have been overly bothered about it, evidence of their city's Viking past was steadily building, accumulating in London's national and civic collections (the British Museum and the forerunners to the Museum of London).

In the 1880s a Viking sword was unveiled with the dubious – though rather exciting – claim that it had been recovered from the tomb of Gilbert de Clare, first earl of Pembroke (d.1148), in Temple Church. A fine blade of pattern-welded steel, its hilt inlaid with copper serpents, bound with silver wire, it came to London by means unknown to be lost or buried there: a relic of a time when the city's future was being moulded by the presence of Scandinavians and the aftershocks of their coming. The sword remains in the city, hanging now in the British Museum on public display. The remains of London's Viking Age endure within the city – the weapons dragged from the Thames and the runestone erected by Ginna and Toki, the fragments of ship-timbers and Danish metalwork plucked from the waterfront, the buried spoils of Viking terror and the coins that were hidden from them, the dedications to St Olaf, the footings of homes, of streets and workshops – the tangible, physical manifestation of a past that has shaped one of the greatest cities in the world.

Notes, sources
and further reading

This volume was written in the wake of the publication of my book *Viking Britain* in 2017 (William Collins), and while each may stand entirely alone, the two books complement each other. *Viking Britain* provides the wider context for the history explored here, and also elaborates topics which, for reasons of space, have not received full treatment in *Viking London*. Conversely, this book adopts a tight focus which the earlier book could not; in doing so, I hope, it presents new perspectives on the impact of the Vikings in Britain. It also explores more fully the half-century after Cnut's accession in 1016, a period which *Viking Britain* touched on only briefly.

Viking London is not intended to be a comprehensive analysis of London's Viking Age history and archaeology; nor is it an academic textbook or a guide to the scholarly literature pertaining to the subject. In recognition of this, I have endeavoured to keep the text as unencumbered as possible, and notes have been used to indicate sources cited or specifically referred to in the text, as well as to provide a few additional comments and clarifications. The most commonly used primary sources are referred to by abbreviation, and a list of these is provided below. Otherwise, full bibliographic details are provided in the notes. Citations from and references to the manuscripts of the *Anglo-Saxon Chronicle* have made use of the editions published under the general supervision of David Dumville and Simon Keynes (see individual volumes below). Where a reference to the *Chronicle* is given in the notes simply as *ASC*, the material cited is common to all manuscripts (the 'common stock'); otherwise, references specify the manuscript by letter when information is restricted to one or more versions. Translations from the *Chronicle* and from Old English and Old Norse poetry are my own unless otherwise indicated. In all other cases, primary sources cited in the text are taken from the translated editions listed below.

There are, of course, a number of other published works on which I have relied but which are not systematically referred to. Of these, a few key publications stand out as being of particular importance to the subject, and to them I owe a significant debt. By far the most readable and up-to-date treatment of early medieval London is Rory Naismith's *Citadel of the Saxons* (2018, I.B. Tauris) – essential reading for anyone interested in the broad sweep of the city's development in this period. Naismith's book is also well served with maps and direction to the relevant scholarly literature. (I am extremely grateful to Dr Naismith for making the draft manuscript of his book available to me prior to its publication.) Older, but still extremely valuable, general works on London's early medieval past include *London 800–1216: The Shaping of a City* by Christopher Brooke with Gillian Keir (1975, University of California Press) and *Saxon London: An Archaeological Investigation* by Alan Vince (1990, Seaby).

For the archaeology of Lundenwic, the reader should consult *Lundenwic: Excavations in Middle Saxon London 1987–2000* by Robert Cowie and Lyn Blackmore, with Anne Davis, Jackie Keily and Kevin Rielly (2012, Museum of London Archaeology). This hefty book is a treasury of material relating to all aspects of the development of the early settlement. There is currently no comparable volume dealing with the archaeology of Lundenburh, but *The Development of Early Medieval and Later Poultry and Cheapside: Excavations at 1 Poultry and Vicinity, City of London* by Mark Burch and Phil Treveil with Derek Keene (2011, Museum of London Archaeology), though more specifically focused on the excavations named in the title, is also invaluable for the archaeology of Lundenburh more widely. Important excavations at Guildhall are covered in *The London Guildhall: An Archaeological History of a Neighbourhood from Early Medieval to Modern Times* by Isca Howell, David Bowsher, Tony Dyson and Nick Holder (2012, Museum of London Archaeology). The MOLA-produced *The Archaeology of Greater London* (2007, Museum of London Archaeology) contains several important chapters and is currently free to download from the MOLA website (mola.org.uk/publications). Two important book-length 'special papers' – *Aspects of Saxo-Norman London I: Buildings and Street Development* by Valerie

Horsman, Christine Milne and Gustav Milne (1988, LAMAS), and *Aspects of Saxo-Norman London II: Finds and Environmental Evidence* by Alan Vince (1991, LAMAS) – published by the London and Middlesex Archaeological Society (LAMAS) – are also free to access (lamas.org.uk/archives/special-papers).

A number of individual papers stand out as being of particular importance. A. Dyson, 'King Alfred and the restoration of London', *London Journal* 15:2 (1990), pp. 99–110; R. Naismith, 'London and its mint *c*.880–1066: a preliminary survey', *British Numismatic Journal* 83 (2013), pp. 44–74; J. Ayre and R. Wroe-Brown, 'The Eleventh- and twelfth-century waterfront and settlement at Queenhithe: excavations at Bull Wharf, City of London', *Archaeological Journal* 172 (2015), pp. 195–272; V. Zeigler, 'From *wic* to *burh*: a new approach to the question of the development of Early Medieval London', *Archaeological Journal* 176 (2019). I am very grateful to Andrew Reynolds for giving me sight of the chapter 'London in the Age of Cnut' which is set to appear in a forthcoming collection concerning the reign of Cnut (edited by Richard North) and is much to be recommended.

Abbreviations and notes

AB

> *The Annals of St-Bertin*, s.a. 847; J. Nelson (ed. and trans.), *The Annals of St-Bertin* (1991, Manchester University Press)

AC

> *Annales Cambriae*; J. Morris (ed.), *Nennius, British History and the Welsh Annals* (1980, Phillimore)

ASC

> *Anglo-Saxon Chronicle* (see above);

> A
>
> > J.M. Bately (ed.), *The Anglo-Saxon Chronicle: A Collaborative Edition, vol. 3. MS. A* (1986, Brewer)

> C
>
> > K. O'Brien O'Keeffe (ed.), *The Anglo-Saxon Chronicle: A Collaborative Edition, vol. 5. MS. C* (2001, Brewer)

D

G.P. Cubbin (ed.), *The Anglo-Saxon Chronicle: A Collaborative Edition, vol. 6. MS. D* (1996, Brewer)

E

S. Irvine (ed.), *The Anglo-Saxon Chronicle: A Collaborative Edition, vol. 7. MS. E:* (2004, Brewer)

ASPR

Anglo-Saxon Poetic Records; G.P. Krapp and E.V. Dobbie, (eds), 1931–53, *The Anglo-Saxon poetic records: a collective edition*, 6 vols, New York: Columbia University Press [ota.ox.ac.uk/desc/1936]

AU

Annals of Ulster; University College Cork: *Corpus of Electronic Texts (CELT)* [celt.ucc.ie//published/T100001A]

CA

Æthelweard, *'Chronicon' of Æthelweard*; A. Campbell (ed. and trans.), *The Chronicle of Æthelweard* (1962, Thomas Nelson & Sons)

Carmen

Guy of Amiens. *Carmen de Hastingae Proelio*; F. Barlow (ed. and trans.), *Carmen de Hastingae Proelio of Guy, Bishop of Amiens* (1999, Oxford University Press)

CC

John of Worcester, *Chronicon ex Chronicis*; R.R. Darlington (ed.), P. McGurk (ed. and trans.) and J. Bray (trans.), *The Chronicle of John of Worcester* (1995, Clarendon Press)

EHD

English Historical Documents; D. Whitelock, *English Historical Documents 500–1041*, Vol I (1979 [2nd edition], Routledge)

Enc.

Anon., *Encomium Emmae Reginae*; A. Campbell (ed. and tr.) and S. Keynes, *Encomium Emmae Reginae* (1998, Cambridge University Press)

HE

Bede, *Historia Ecclesiastica Gentis Anglorum*; D.H. Farmer (ed. and trans.) and L. Sherley-Price (trans.), *Ecclesiastical History of the English People* (1991, Penguin)

Heimskringla II

Snorri Sturluson, *Heimskringla*; A. Finlay and A. Faulkes (eds and trans.), *Heimskringla Volume II: Óláfr Haraldsson (The Saint)* (2014, Viking Society for Northern Research)

Liðsmannaflokkr

Anon., *Liðsmannaflokkr*; R.G. Poole, *Viking Poems on War and Peace: A Study in Skaldic Narrative* (1991, University of Toronto Press), pp. 86–115

S

Charter number assigned in P.H. Sawyer, *Anglo-Saxon Charters: An Annotated List and Bibliography* (1968, Royal Historical Society); details and additional bibliographical information available online at esawyer. org.uk

Saga-book:
  Saga-book of the Viking Society[/*Club*]

VA
  Asser, *Vita Ælfredi Regis Angul Saxonum*; S. Keynes
  and M. Lapidge, *Alfred the Great: Asser's 'Life of King
  Alfred' and Other Contemporary Sources* (1983,
  Penguin Classics)

Chapter I: Lundenwic

1   *ASC* s.a. 842
2   *AB* s.a. 842
3   S 134
4   *HE* II.3
5   *Ibid.*
6   *HE* I.29
7   *HE* II.7
8   S 168
9   *The Ruin*, lns.1–9 (*ASPR* 3)
10 J.R.R. Tolkien, 'The Monsters and the Critics' (1936), in C.
    Tolkien (ed.), *The Monsters and the Critics and Other Essays*
    (1997, HarperCollins), p. 23
11 S 670
12 W.H. Black, 'Observations on the recently discovered Roman
    sepulchre at Westminster Abbey', *Transactions of the London
    and Middlesex Archaeological Society* 4 (1871), pp. 60–9
13 S 903
14 S 670
15 H. Melville [H. Harrison (ed.)], *Journals* (1989, Northwestern
    University Press)

16   H. Melville [L. Horth (ed.)], *Correspondence* (1993, North-
      western University Press), p. 205
17   Melville, *Journals*
18   Freely adapted from Dorothy Whitelock's translation from
      the original Latin ('as for the black stones which your
      Reverence begged to be sent to you, let a messenger come
      and consider what kind you have in mind, and we will
      willingly order them to be given, wherever they are to be
      found, and will help with their transport. But as you have
      intimated your wishes concerning the length of the stones,
      so our people make a demand about the size of the cloaks,
      that you may order them to be such as used to come to us
      in former times'); *EHD* 197.
19   *ASC* s.a. 851

Chapter II: Lundenburh

1   T. Dyson, 'King Alfred and the Restoration of London', *The
      London Journal* 15:2 (1990), pp. 99–110, at p. 100
2   S 1278; *EHD* 94
3   I. Sinclair, *The Last London* (2017, Oneworld), p. 292
4   *Ibid.*, p. 290
5   'Beowulf', l. 104 (*ASPR* 4)
6   S 1628
7   *ASC* s.a. 886
8   *Anglo-Saxon Dictionary*; J. Bosworth and T. Toller, *An Anglo-
      Saxon Dictionary* (1898, Clarendon Press), T. Toller, *An
      Anglo-Saxon Dictionary: Supplement* (1921, Clarendon Press)
9   Amongst other evidence for the ongoing status of Mercian
      rulers, the tenth-century Mercian chronicler and aristocrat
      Æthelweard referred to Æthelred as *rex* ('king'), and his
      wife, Alfred's daughter Æthelflæd, was likewise referred to

as a queen by Irish and Welsh chroniclers. *CA*, p. 51; *AC* s.a. 917; *AU* s.a. 918.

10   *ASC* E s.a. 883
11   Beginning with *ASC* s.a. 851
12   *VA* 91
13   *Ibid.*
14   *Ibid.*
15   S 208
16   S 346 and 1628
17   H. Melville, *Moby-Dick or, The Whale* (1851, Penguin Classics 2003), p. xxxix
18   N. Lund (ed.) and C. Fell (trans.), *Two Voyagers at the Court of King Alfred* (1984, William Sessions), p. 18; my translation.
19   *ASC* s.a. 894
20   *Ibid.*
21   *ASC* s.a. 896
22   *ASC* s.a. 913
23   *ASC* A s.a. 916; C, D s.a. 914
24   *ASC* D s.a. 968; *EHD* 4
25   *ASC* A 962

Chapter III: Lundúnir

1   *The Battle of Maldon*, ASPR 6
2   *ASC* CDE s.a. 992
3   *ASC* CDE s.a. 994
4   *ASC* CDE s.a. 1009
5   J. Conrad, *Heart of Darkness* (1899, Penguin Classics 2007), p. 5
6   *ASC* CDE s.a. 1012
7   I. Sinclair, *Lud Heat: A Book of the Dead Hamlets* (1975, Skylight Press 2012)

8 *ASC* CDE s.a. 1012

9 VI Athelstan, *EHD* 38

10 *Ibid.*

11 *ASC* CDE s.a. 1013

12 *Elene, ASPR* 2, 41–6, 121–3); prose translation of Old English verse by S.A.J. Bradley, *Anglo-Saxon Poetry* (1982, Everyman), p. 168

13 *ASC* CDE s.a. 1016

14 *ASC* CDE s.a. 1013

15 *ASC* CDE s.a. 1016

16 *Ibid.*

17 *Enc.* 4, pp. 18–21

18 S. Sturluson (trans. M. Magnusson and H. Pálsson), *King Harald's Saga* (1966, Penguin 2005)

19 D.H. Hill, 'The Burghal Hidage – the establishment of a text', Medieval Archaeology 13 (1969), pp. 84–92

20 *Heimskringla II*, ch. 12, p. 10

21 *ASC* CDE s.a. 1016; *Enc.* 7, pp. 22–3

22 *Helgisaga Óláfs konungs Haraldssonar* ('The Legendary Saga'), *Flateyjarbók* and *Knýtlinga saga*

23 *Liðsmannaflokkr*, stanzas 2, 4, 7

24 *Ibid.*, stanza 9

25 *Ibid.*, stanza 10

Chapter IV: Lundúnaborg

1 *CC*, s.a. 1017

2 *ASC* D s.a. 1023

3 R. Morris and A. Rumble (trans.), 'Textual Appendix: "Translatio sancti Ælfegi Cantuariensis archiepiscopi et martiris" ', in A. Rumble (ed.), *The Reign of Cnut: King of England, Denmark and Norway* (1994, Leicester University Press), pp. 283–315

4   O. Elton (trans.), *The Nine Books of the Danish History of Saxo Grammaticus* (1905, Norroena Society), Book 1

5   Rundata DR 337 (Scandinavian Runic-text Database: nordiska.uu.se)

6   *Liðsmannaflokkr*, stanza 10

7   *ASC* D s.a. 1052

8   *Corpus of Anglo-Saxon Stone Sculpture*, Vol. IV, London (St Paul's Cathedral) 01 (ascorpus.ac.uk)

9   *CC* s.a. 1040

10   M. Carlin, *Medieval Southwark* (1996, Hambledon Press), p. 86

11   *Heimskringla II*, ch. 12, p. 10

12   *Ibid.*, ch. 13, p. 10

13   Ottarr svarti, *Hofuðlausn* (translation from M. O. Townend, *English Place-Names in Skaldic Verse* (1998, English Place-Name Society)

14   *ASC* E s.a. 1036

15   *ASC* E s.a. 1039

16   *CC* s.a. 1040

17   *ASC* C s.a. 1040

18   'De Miraculis Sancti Eadmundi, by Hermannus the Archdeacon', in T. Arnold (ed.), *Memorials of St Edmund's Abbey*, 3 vols (1890–9, Rolls Series), Vol. I, p. 54

19   *ASC* D s.a. 1052

20   *Carmen*, pp. 38–9

21   *Ibid.*

22   M. Chibnall (ed. and trans.), *The Ecclesiastical History of Orderic Vitalis*, 6 vols (1968–80, Clarendon Press), Vol. II, pp. 184–5

23   J. Conrad, *Heart of Darkness* (1899, Penguin Classics 2007), p. 5

Chapter V: Vikings Drink Tea

1 J.A.B. Townend, 'The Viking Society: A Centenary History', *Saga-book* XXIII (1990–3), pp. 180–212; p. 180

2 *Ibid.*, p. 183

3 *Saga-book* I (1893–6), p. 1

4 *Pall Mall Gazette* (15 January 1894), p. 7

5 *Ibid.*

6 'Reports of the Proceedings at the Meetings of the Club; Third Session, 1895', *Saga-book* I (1893–6), pp. 120–57; p. 141

7 'Reports of the Proceedings at the Meetings of the Club; First Session, 1892–3', *Saga-book* I (1893–6), pp. 5–41; p. 24

8 *Ibid.* p. 27

9 A.H. Cocks, 'A Boat Journey to Inari', *Saga-book* I (1893–6), pp. 319–49; p. 348

10 'Reports of the Proceedings at the Meetings of the Club; First Session, 1892–3', *Saga-book* I (1893–6), pp. 5–41; p. 37

11 Adapted from 'Reports of the Proceedings at the Meetings of the Club; Third Session, 1895', *Saga-book* I (1893–6), pp. 120–57; p. 120

12 'Death-roll', *Saga-book* I (1893–6), pp. 286–8; p. 287

13 L. Greenlaw, *Questions of Travel: William Morris in Iceland* (2011, Notting Hill Editions)

Index

Many thanks are due to Dr Rory Naismith (King's College London), Professor Andrew Reynolds (UCL) and Dr Gareth Williams and my other friends and former colleagues at the British Museum for their help, advice and good cheer. I am also grateful to my editors at William Collins and to Julian Alexander and Ben Clark at the Soho Agency for all of their assistance. The support of my family has been critical to the successful completion of this project. I owe a particular debt to my father Geoffrey, for – amongst other things – his patient and insightful reading of this manuscript as it evolved over several versions. I thank him for his indefatigability. I take responsibility for any errors that remain; idiosyncrasies and neologisms are, however, probably deliberate.